To George Mardikian
whose hospitality and
love of America warmed
my heart at Omar
Khayyam's January 15, 1965.

Edward S. [illegible]

This Before Architecture

EDWARD S. FREY, D.D.

Executive Director
Commission on Church Architecture
Lutheran Church in America

Introduction by

Harold E. Wagoner, A.I.A.

1963

FOUNDATION BOOKS
Jenkintown, Pennsylvania

THE RELIGIOUS PUBLISHING COMPANY
122 Old York Road
Jenkintown, Pa.

Library of Congress Card Catalog No. 63-14304

First Printing

PRINTED IN THE UNITED STATES OF AMERICA

PRESS OF H. RAY HAAS & CO.
ALLENTOWN, PENNSYLVANIA

CONTENTS

ILLUSTRATIONS

INTRODUCTION

It is a mistake to believe that Churches are designed by architects. They are, in reality, ultimately shaped by public opinion, rough hewn by a concert in which the pastor, the building committee, the congregation and the architect play fluctuating roles. But public opinion in itself does not grow spontaneously. It is the result of controlled, and uncontrolled, forces.

As Director of the Commission on Church Architecture, Lutheran Church in America, Dr. Edward S. Frey in *This Before Architecture* channels the whimsical, and often erratic forces which determine the character of religious structures, into a rational set of tenets which serve as guideposts to sensible church building in a changing world.

It could be fairly said that the American public has had too little concern over the appropriateness of its religious structures in relation to their worship practices. Our congregations have spent the past 100 years under an aura of rather universal mediocrity in which each church has vied with its neighbor to produce a gentle and inoffensive church architecture, sometimes sweet and urban, sometimes nostalgic and sentimental. Dr. Frey points to the fact that this is the natural result of the congregation's failure to understand its individual purposes and its individual program. "Think! Before you build," epitomizes the whole tenor of his philosophy. "Building committees frequently . . . start at the wrong end of their job. They begin busily with the problems of architecture. What will the building look like? Where will it be placed on the site? How much will it cost?"

He goes on to say: "The first question in a building program is — what do we believe about God and why has He called us together in this place to do His work? — This is where we begin, not with architecture or finance."

Dr. Frey is a native of York, Pennsylvania. Following his graduation from Gettysburg Lutheran Theological Seminary, he spent 16 years as pastor of Trinity Lutheran Church in Lemoyne, Pennsylvania.

When Dr. Frey was appointed Executive Secretary of the Department of Church Architecture of the United Lutheran Church in America, I can remember mumbling to myself, "Can any good thing come out of Lemoyne?" (I have never been in Lemoyne, but it could be fairly said, I think, that it was not noted for its architecture. Doubtless there are good buildings there.) Well, I suppose there was a time when Emporia, Kansas — and maybe even Bethlehem — were not too well known. Something good *did* come from Lemoyne.

From the beginning, Dr. Frey clearly understood the major reasons why American Churches failed to measure up to their European counterparts; namely, a lack of understanding among the clergy and laity as to their worship practices. He has this to say: "The program of the Church whose people will not think under God, takes on bit by bit the mores of the secular groups that surround it, bidding for attention — badges and buttons, banners, bingo and bake sales, and a theology witless and anemic, with no power to save . . . I have visited many buildings in which the kitchen is the best planned room . . . What can one believe about this, other than that the congregation understands better what goes on in the kitchen than what is meant to happen in the sanctuary or classroom."

In his new post as Director of the destinies of Lutheran Architecture in America, Dr. Frey's abilities were immediately recognized by his colleagues, and by the church architects with whom he came in contact. In addition to his other duties he was appointed chairman of the Board of Managers of the Department of Church Building and Architecture of the National Council of Churches. In this position, through his lectures and writings, and through his prodigious efforts in the Lutheran Department of Church Architecture, his influence was felt far beyond the limits of his own denomination.

There are many American church architects (such as the undersigned) who can speak with an appreciable amount of first hand knowledge of this influence. American church architecture has changed more in the past 5 years, than in the preceding 30. A great deal of this change can, I think, be directly and indirectly attributed to the continuous effort of Dr. Frey to promote the theory that "Architecture is the business of the architect; the description of the Church's life and purpose, what it believes, and what is proposes to do about it, is the business of the congregation . . . The analysis of worship that would be most relevant and fruitful for the architect would be that which deals with worship as an activity, rather than as an idea or mental image."

Dr. Frey should not be looked upon so much as a prophet as he should be regarded as a leader who, through great conviction in the things in which he believes, has been able to persuade vast numbers of religious people to think before they act. He wants to avoid the kind of church which has the "preacher and choir as a kind of permanent cast, addressing the passive people in the pews."

This is not a book about architecture, but a book about architecture as a by-product of the introspective probing of Building Committee and congregation. Nor is it a plea for "modern" architecture (except by indirection). " . . . I see new abominations in the making, the direct result of architectural exhibitionism with its egocentric rather than theocentric motivations . . . 'Costume' architecture won't work."

Every pastor would do well to read *This Before Architecture* carefully, and to see to it that his building committee echoes this task. Every architect who has been commissioned to design a church, should send this book to his clients, after he himself has read and understood its message. Dr. Frey focuses one's attention on principles of approach to church architecture, and refrains from the obvious pitfall of drawing material conclusions which could have nullified the excellent effect of mental stimulation.

"Architecture, good architecture, is the end result," he says, "*not* the starting point for a successful building program."

Harold E. Wagoner, A.I.A.
Past President, Church Architectural Guild of America
President, Philadelphia Chapter, American Institute of Architects

Philadelphia, Pennsylvania
February 15, 1963

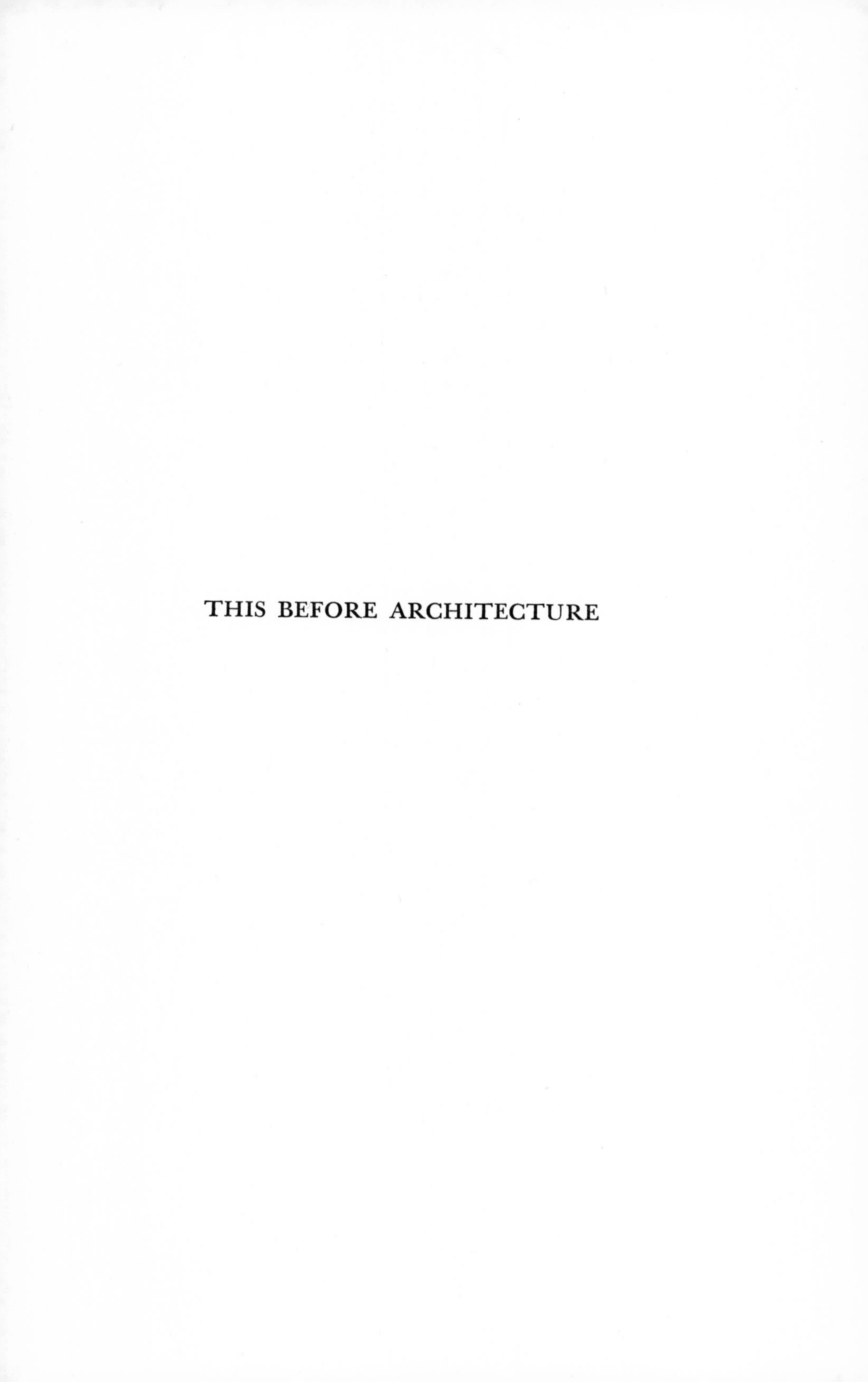

THIS BEFORE ARCHITECTURE

TO MARIA

and

the many good friends
who inspired these
lectures

1

THE ROLE OF THEOLOGY IN CHURCH ARCHITECTURE

This address was delivered in Troy, New York, May 1, 1957, during a conference on church architecture sponsored by the Department of Architecture, Renssalaer Polytechnic Institute and the Department of Church Building and Architecture, National Council of Churches. Though this address was delivered chiefly to architects, it has many specific values and points of information for pastors and church building committees.

The Role of Theology in Church Architecture

SUCCESS in building, especially for worship, depends largely upon where and how you begin. And, you don't begin with architecture! Of course, there comes a time in the building program when there must be architectural thinking, but this is not at the beginning.

At the beginning of building for worship, everyone should be a theologian. I need not tell you, however, that this is rarely the case. Usually, everyone tries to be an architect or some sort of financier. The congregation and the architect must first be concerned with *program* and not architecture. What is the purpose of the building they are to build? Who is He whom we worship, and what is worship? These are the questions that must be answered and the business of answering them is the first thing on the agenda of the building program.

It may be that the following story is apocryphal, but I do not think so. I heard it a long time ago. Dr. Joseph Sittler's article in a recent issue of the *Christian Century*[1] brought it to my attention again.

[1] Joseph Sittler, "A Hammer, the Incarnation and Architecture," *The Christian Century* (March 27, 1957), p. 394.

The story deals with the beginnings of an outstanding contemporary church building. The building committee, as is so often the case, had just about designed their new church building when they called in their architect. He laid aside their efforts as courteously as possible and said to them directly, "Now just what do you people really believe?"

Not what the building is to look like; *not* its size or its cost — *but,* exactly what is it and what is it to do, are the first questions to be considered and finally answered before a line is drawn on paper. For five years, I have fought an uphill battle on this front and in a denomination that knows better than some that these are the chief desiderata. I sometimes wonder how my brothers in this field in those denominations that are less firm in their liturgies are able to stand the gaff.

THEOLOGY BEFORE ARCHITECTURE

So, *program* comes before building, *theology* comes before architecture, and *informed conviction* as to the precise task of the congregation in worship comes before the form and furnishings of the room for worship!

If you are not interested in theology; that is to say, if you have no specifically Christian conviction of your own or are not challenged by such conviction in others, don't take a church job! The courage of conviction is so necessary; and, the courage not to compromise your art. Without conviction and courage, the result is very apt to be a nave and chancel that will be merely imitative and for that reason somewhat phony, certainly not representative of the congregation's best intentions.

Of course, being a "practical theologian" will not make you an architectural genius — it may even cramp your style — but your building will have sincerity, will be a good tool in the service of the church and her Lord.

Now, it would seem that unless I were to stop right here, having stated my principal theses, that the thing to do is to talk a bit about some questions that must have been raised in your minds.

Have I gone too far? Am I making too much of having to know about the church and its people before it is possible to put together a building that will represent its life and be useful to its purpose? I don't think so.

What is expected of you in designing a church? The really unique area in the church building complex is the church room; i.e., nave, chancel, and sanctuary. The requirements will always be unusual and you will have to grasp the unique occasion. This will take study — yours and the congregation's. The opportunity for creative design is unlimited. The difference here between this and all other kinds of building is immense. The *Difference* must be spoken for and served by you. It is too much! If you are an honest man, you will admit it. But, being a man, and this being your job, you will try it. You will not be able to begin intelligently or honestly unless you know as many of the implications of what you are doing as it is possible to know.

The least you have got to know is what the people believe about God and His worship. And from the very beginning, you have got to be under the conviction, whether the people are or not, that this is God's House.

> If, then, it is really God's House and not merely a convenient place in which to worship Him, any

> true architectural expression must recognize the qualities and character of the real owner. If someone builds a house for me and builds it without recognizing anything of my character and tastes, to say the least, he is an unfaithful steward of my funds. To build the house of God and make beauty, dignity and spirituality, as expressed in architecture, entirely secondary to good heating and acoustics, is to build God's House without God.[2]

Let us say it again. It is God's House you are to design when you are commissioned to build a church. A. G. Hebert has come as close perhaps as a man can to saying what this means, what a church building as God's House is.

> The church building and the liturgical acts performed there express something about Christianity which the preacher's words can never give. We hear him preach, and we say he is a holy man, or a clever man, or maybe the reverse. If the church service consisted of preachings, we should conclude that the Church was a religious movement. But you cannot sum up as merely the home of a religious movement the building where baptisms, weddings, and funerals are celebrated – not to speak of the rest. It is the home of the people, the house of God. It speaks of a real and permanent relation of God with men. It witnesses to a truth deeper and greater than the truth of human beliefs and ideas – the truth of that which underlies man's own existence, the Source and Ground of all Being.[3]

UNDER THE DISCIPLINE OF THE LITURGY

Building for worship must be under the discipline of the liturgy which your design is to serve. This is

[2] Von Ogden Vogt, *Art and Religion* (Boston, 1948), p. 236.
[3] A. G. Hebert, *Liturgy and Society* (London, 1956), p. 41.

to say that the design of the church room must spring from the theology and practice of the corporate worship of the congregation. Let this be the controlling consideration and you will have a ready handle for most of the problems, I would say for all the serious ones, that will arise in respect to the planning of the church room. I should like to illustrate the importance of this. Some weeks ago, I was chairing the sessions of a workshop held in connection with the National Joint Conference on Church Architecture held in St. Louis. The theme of the workshop was "The Choir — Its Contribution and Location." Looking back to these sessions I find myself still amazed at the fact that not more than one person in five seemed to have ever realized before that *the studied purpose of the church choir in worship must be the first consideration in locating it.* I know this was so because I could see it on the faces of the participants. When it came to them that the central problem in placing the choir is theological and not musical, or traditional, or ministerial, or theatrical, or acoustical, they either changed their tune at once, so as not to be left behind, and came awake with the spirit of adventure or, they went warmly on the defensive in the hope that they could conceal the fact that their prepared positions were built on sand. I am speaking latterly of those who were prepared to support the location of their choirs with reasons that were less than theological. What we think about worship will, of course, lead us to a statement of the purpose of the choir in the activity of corporate worship.

Literally, there is no other way to arrive at the proper location or architectural character of any element in the ground plan without a previous statement of its meaning for the corporate worship of the church.

Any approach short of this will certainly lead to a disorderly design. Certain elements will assume a prominence which is not their due and others of equal or greater significance will be slighted. In the closing hours of the St. Louis workshop, rough floor plans were drawn on the chalkboard to illustrate some possible choir location solutions. Still not fully realizing the fundamental necessity of taking into account the primary theological considerations, a few of these drawings made it appear that the church building was created mainly to house the choir.

When your services are sought by a congregation, you will do them and yourself good and your work will be made somewhat easier if you urge them to contact their denominational agency concerned with building. This is a good procedure whatever the specific architectural problem. You may be sure that this thesis of program definition before architectural planning is shared by all the active denominational agencies.

The agency of my denomination of which I am the director, has a number of helpful publications and services. Let me mention just one thing that we can do in the area of building for worship. We do all we can to encourage the congregation to examine fully its thelogy of worship and to evaluate its present program in the light of its findings.

Now, if the people of the congregation don't know what the church building is to do in addition to providing shelter and seating and are unwilling to stir themselves to find out, the architect will have to do all in his power beyond his normal function of designing to guide them. Here, too, help can be had from the denominational agencies that are in business to counsel in these things. If there is no denominational agency for the congregation you are serving, the Department of Church Building and Architecture of the National Council of Churches can be called upon.

There is very little difference today between one and another of the basic tenets of the great churches of Protestantism. The doctrinal differences that exist arise mostly out of varying emphasis. In certain doctrines, the variation of emphasis is considerable and nearly always evident in the pattern of worship. To return again for an example to the St. Louis workshop, everyone was in general agreement as to the primary purpose of the choir, but it became apparent early in the discussion that two widely divergent concepts of the choir's function were held by the participants, each with its variants having a great deal to do with the problem of design for corporate worship. The concepts were: (1) the choir was a ministry, an adjunct of the clergy which, with the clergy, ministers to the congregation; and (2) the choir was a part of the congregation which, though it may lead in the musical responses and hymns and sometimes alone render a musical offering to God, has no independent place in the service of worship.

One can hardly conceive of two views of the same thing farther apart than these. Yet, scattered among the congregations, there are divergencies of this nature that bear heavily upon design in nearly every element of importance in the liturgy as well as in the minor services. Even among congregations within the same denomination, variations and divergencies of emphasis and practice occur. Of course, this poses problems for the architect, but it is also his exciting challenge.

But, deep underneath, everywhere among all Christian churches, there are, shall we say, "major characteristics" which no building for worship can be without and at the same time succeed as a building.

CHARACTERISTICS OF SUCCESSFUL CHURCH ARCHITECTURE

Let us devote what remains of our time to an attempt to name some of these characteristics. The appearance of the church building inside and out should be such as to leave no one in doubt that its chief function is to express and promote the Christian relationship between God and man. If this is so, three distinguishing characteristics will mark the building. It will be (a) theologically correct, (b) ecclesiastically proper, (c) characteristically true of the One we worship.

THEOLOGICALLY CORRECT

Architecturally speaking, this means that every object that meets the eye must belong to the high purpose of the room. The room must possess unity and all objects, decoration, and arrangements must be such as to preserve that unity. The architecture must emphasize the action of the liturgy. This must be so because the liturgy of the church is the expression of its faith celebrated in the corporate worship of the congregation.

The building must possess strength and beauty in a form appropriate to its peculiar task — a witness to member and non-member alike of the honor in which He is held by the congregation who erects this building to His glory and as a witness to His continuing presence with His people. The building would not be theologically correct if it were badly situated, poorly designed, too cheaply or too expensively built. (Better the plan be incomplete but done well than be complete but of flimsy construction and indifferent design.)

Painting and sculpture should be reclaimed by the architect for their service to the church. The witnessing function of the arts is not a mere decorative function. The function of the arts in the service of the church as I believe Emil Brunner has said is to open the way for the Word to enter the soul, to intensify the impression made by the Word of the Scriptures and the proclamation of the Gospel.

Dr. Joseph Sittler has written[4] that the Christian proclamation, *The Word Became Flesh and Dwelt Among Us,* puts one at the central place for pondering what the form of a Christian church should announce. Therefore "what should be celebrated in both architecture and [worship] is not general religiousness, unspecified spirituality, or a miasmic if potent mood of sheer otherness." This means, of course, that church building is a religious act celebrating a present fact — the announcement and reality that it is the Christian faith that God's revelation of Himself is bound to time and place.

ECCLESIASTICALLY PROPER

The building should provide a proper material and esthetic setting for the task of the congregation and its worship. It should be so planned as to make every provision for the orderly gathering together of the people in response to the Gospel, to magnify the means of grace and to surround every liturgical action and general activity with decency, order, and beauty.

How this would detail itself in some churches, I don't know; but in a Lutheran church these principles

[4] *Architectural Record* (Dec., 1955), pp. 190-1

would find expression in ample aisles, clear foci to all principal points, an altar-centered axis, pulpit significant, font, if not monumental, at least permanent and in plain sight, and every reasonable provision for an orderly celebration of the Lord's Supper at the altar with freedom of movement.

In reference to determining what is ecclesiastically proper, notice should be taken of a trend in church building today. It is a recovery of an understanding of worship which was manifested in the thirty years of the Reformation but which fell into neglect during the passing centuries and was supplanted by a romantic understanding of the Church's history and pattern of worship which developed in the 19th century.

Dr. Marvin Halverson, Executive Director of the National Council's Department of Worship and the Arts, has written that recently the liturgical research, Biblical study, and theological inquiry regarding the nature of the church are bringing to a focus the understanding of the Church as a place to fulfill its divine vocation of worshipping God and glorifying Him before the world. "When this is done," he says, "you have an emphasis upon the Holy Table around which the faithful gather to celebrate the family meal, and an emphasis upon every corporate experience of the group in the action of the liturgy." [5]

My own thinking has recently reflected this trend in that I have come to question the propriety, symbolically and liturgically, of the typical and venerable basilican floor plan. As a result, I have come to feel that some form of central plan with its emphasis upon the altar and the priesthood of believers has much to

[5] Marvin Halverson, "On Getting Good Architecture for the Church," in *Religious Buildings for Today*, ed. by John Knox Shear (New York, 1957), p. 5.

1

EPISCOPAL CHURCH OF THE GOOD SHEPHERD

Lyndhurst, Ohio — Ruth & Hayes, A.I.A., Architects

2

LUTHERAN CHURCH OF THE ATONEMENT
Chicago, Illinois

Cooley and Borre, A.I.A.
Architects

3

ST. TIMOTHY'S LUTHERAN CHURCH
Allentown, Pennsylvania

Wolf & Hahn, A.I.A., Architects

4

5

KINGSBURY CONGREGATIONAL COMMUNITY CHURCH
Vernal, Utah Burtch W. Beall, Jr., A.I.A., Architect

6

7

ST. MARK'S EPISCOPAL CHURCH

New Canaan, Connecticut

Sherwood, Mills, and Smith, A.I.A., Architects

recommend itself to Lutherans. It seems to me theologically correct and ecclesiastically proper. At any rate, it is interesting and instructive to think about. I am not necessarily advocating it. Here are some considerations in its favor:

> Altar in "the midst of the people" . . . This does not necessarily mean in the geometrical center of the plan. The perennial choir problem is neatly disposed of . . . It becomes, in a central plan, distinctly a part of the worshipping congregation.
>
> Favorable to the kind of preaching that many of us cherish – not declamatory, oratorical, *but* expository, instructive, pastoral.
>
> Should result in greater participation in the service . . . the distance between the pastor and the people is narrowed down. In the prayers and other liturgical actions surrounding the Lord's Supper with the minister facing the congregation "over" the altar, the instructive items in the prayer and the rite are highlighted.
>
> The sense of community is magnified, the corporate nature of the church, the body of believers . . . all elements of the congregation are together with a common center visually as well as liturgically.

To secure these advantages, it is not necessary to have the altar-table in the true center of the floor plan. Circular, polygonal, square or nearly square areas with the table placed near one of the sides will do it very well.

The church room in any event is not an auditorium. It is something entirely unique and this must be evident. The singing here is no concert; the preaching is no lecture. This is the place of a unique encounter. The Christian worshipper is met before One who manifested Himself in time, the Word become flesh, who is here in His house as a Presence and not simply as an idea. If there is any audience in this room, that audience is God, as Kierkegaard has suggested.

CHARACTERISTICALLY TRUE OF THE ONE WE WORSHIP

The building will have beauty and structural honesty and be frankly of our making. It will be of the community but also in dialectical relationship to it, pointing to a divine community above. The building's beauty will not be designed primarily as an attraction to the outsider, though it will be that in a measure, but as an offering to God.

The building should have something that I call "innocence," by which I mean that it should not be self-conscious. It must not seem to over-reach itself. It must be without pomposity. Such a building would fail to be characteristically true of the One we worship. This quality is to be thought of as in opposition to display, Baroque elegance, or architectural virtuosity, lest the building seem an end in itself and thus conceal God.

In architectural terms, this means there should be a good reason for every detail of design, no decoration for its own sake. It means sincerity in structure, no faking in anything. Any representational art should be of the kind that is a starting place for one's thinking and not a stopping place and that once you have seen it, you have not seen *all* there is.

The building should have life inside and out. It must not look only into the past as if to suggest that it belongs there. It must suggest that its reason for being is relevant now and it must announce a great expectancy for we are a people of hope and our God shall make all things new.

As a last word, let us remember that the principal criteria of a successful church building are theological rather than architectural. It cannot be said too often that there is no such thing, really, as church architecture — there is only architecture in the service of the church. To design for worship is to create a building that is both a symbol and a tool for the worshipping congregation. Success in building for worship stems from the happy marriage of sound theology and skillful, dedicated architecture.

2

WANTED: BETTER BUILDING COMMITTEES

This address has been much edited since it was first delivered at Beverly Hill Community Church, Alexandria, Virginia, May 24, 1958. It was presented there at the National Capital Area Conference on Architecture and Church Building sponsored by the National Capital Area Council of Churches, the Alexandria Council of Churches, and the Department of Church Building and Architecture, National Council of Churches. Under the present title, and much as it appears here, it was published in Protestant Church Buildings and Equipment, *December 1958.*

Wanted: Better Building Committees

A CHURCH building is not an end in itself. It is a symbol and tool in the hands of the Christian congregation for the work of the Lord. Church and parish house buildings are a part of the church's business to witness steadily and clearly to the Gospel.

Ministers and evangelists, missionaries and every dedicated Christian regardless of his place in the church organization is a witness. As a member of the Body of Christ, every man is important. At certain times and at certain places there is a special job of witnessing to be done; for example, when a congregation is faced with a building project. Those active members who for one reason or another seem most competent to discharge this task are appointed by the church. So, for such a member there is added for a time to his daily job of Christian witness a unique opportunity of serving his Lord.

Building committees, however, seem generally to be unaware of their chief responsibilities. Often, much time, effort and funds are wasted because they either do not know or understand what they should do. Often they spend the greater portion of their time attempting to find solutions to architectural problems which they are not competent to solve. As a consequence, their efforts end in frustration or worse.

A prominent architect told me last summer, "I have a hundred letters of appreciation from church clients, my university has honored me with a degree for distinguished service in church architecture, I believe in the Lord Jesus Christ and I love His church but I cannot seem to convince some church building committees that I know a little more than they do about designing and furnishing church buildings. All too often I am asked to design in such fashion as nearly to deny what I believe and to violate fundamental laws of my art."

With good humor, but no less seriously, an architectural consultant once said to me while speaking about the elements of good design, "The great stumbling block to many a good program is the well-intentioned church building committee which is infiltrated with 'fifth columnists of architecture' so that one must use the wiles of a Madame Pompadour, the obliqueness of a Cardinal Richelieu, and the ruthlessness of a munitions salesman in order to guide the congregation to plan and construct a building that is a reasonable response in architecture to what they believe about God and what they want to do about it."

What is needed most today is church building committees better informed as to their true task. Church building is a deliberate, peculiarly powerful and dramatic way of witnessing. In this strange time when the church in some respects has never been so strong and in others so weak, people building churches must know what they do.

It must be understood that, big or little, a building program is a religious act. Building to the glory of

God is an evangelistic enterprise demanding as much intelligence, devotion, Christian faith and stewardship as anything the church of Jesus Christ is ever called to do. A building program deeply affects the whole life of a congregation for generations. The material building is not as important as what is done in it and with it. The daily witness of our faith is first and it is the whole reason for building in the first place.

Building committees frequently do not understand this and start at the wrong end of their job. They begin busily with the problems of architecture. What will the building look like? Where will it be placed on the site? How much will it cost? These are certainly legitimate questions but they can be answered satisfactorily only with the professional help of the experienced architect. Under no condition should committees seek to answer these questions until they have studied the life and purpose of the church and of their church specifically, and its program in the community.

The primary business of the building committee is to discover the living traditions of the church and the congregation's strategy of witness in the community in all the ways that witness is made through worship, education, fellowship and service. The conclusions should be set down in a written "building program." This must be done for the church's own understanding and the architect's guidance. Describing as clearly as possible everything the congregation hopes to do with its new or expanded facilities is the chief business of the building committee.

A church building speaks. What it will say to the community and the world depends upon the studies and the conclusions of the building committee. The edifice may well say less, but it can say no more, than the builders believe.

If our religious thinking is fuzzy and our ideas about the church's ministry are cloudy, our buildings will inevitably reveal it. Lewis Mumford said: "Architecture, like government, is about as good as a community deserves. A shell which we create for ourselves marks our spiritual development as plainly as that of a snail denotes its species." [1] Our church buildings not only reveal what we believe but they are also an indication of what we are.

Dr. Joseph Sittler, a present-day theologian, also said it well: "People are together in response to the Gospel; they have to keep the rain off their heads, enclose the space to keep noise and cold out, arrange the place to sing, speak, teach, behold. Very good. The congregation needs such a building, but there should also be some clear and unsilenceable impulse which leaves us unsatisfied with only that. This listening is not just to a speech; this singing is no concert; this teaching is not just an addition to general education. There is a difference, and one is aware that unless this difference is sharply perceived, clearly defined, realized and announced in material and form, the whole situation stammers its meaning to the world, doesn't speak out clearly. This is why the church, the child and servant of the Gospel, has got to take seriously the planning of its buildings." [2]

This is Dr. Sittler's way of saying that building committees must be able to express to the architect what they know about God. What we believe and all that we want our church to do about it in its building, must be taken into strict account in our planning.

[1] Lewis Mumford, *Sticks and Stones* (New York, 1955), p. 151.
[2] Chicago Lutheran Seminary *Record* (Oct., 1953), pp. 3-4.

Building committees should do their work thoughtfully. They must be as concerned about what the building says as about the space it provides. They should know what the Church is and what its divinely appointed mission is. In the time ahead there will be many temptations to sidestep or forget altogether the real reasons for building. The official board of the church should initiate the building program by taking a searching look at the church in the light of what the church has always believed it should be. Such a study will be disturbing but inspiring.

Vague ideas should never be allowed to determine what we build. Only our earnest convictions about our Christian faith and what we mean to do with these convictions in our church program should determine the form and function of our church buildings. This places squarely upon the shoulders of the building committee the responsibility of raising such questions as these:

1. What is to be the program in Sunday church school as well as in church? What is the whole program in parish education, including teaching, study, teacher-training, fellowship, evangelism?
2. Who are to be *reached?* What are their ages, groupings, and individual needs?
3. What do we need to do in our corporate worship to celebrate more fully and appropriately the presence of our gracious God among his people?
4. What new methods are to be used in our church school program on Sundays and during the week? Which old ones are to be retained and which discarded?
5. What rooms and equipment are believed to be necessary?

Thoughtful committees will be careful committees. The program facts they uncover will be thorough and will represent sound intentions. The result will be a building that is an eloquent witness and one that will support the congregation's program.

Doing the work thoroughly also means that each activity in which the congregation is to be engaged must be seen in its relation to the whole witness of the church. Regardless of the size or extent of the new building, or improvement contemplated, a *complete, thorough program* should be written. For example, if only one unit of a three unit master-plan is to be built now, the work of all the units must be thoroughly described even though two of them may not be built for years. If this is not done, the unit to be first constructed will not serve as well as it might, either now or in the future.

Building committees must serve unselfishly. I can't think of anything a congregation does as a body that is more unselfish than to complete a successful building program. It is a mathematical certainty that the return to us when we build cannot equal the benefit that hundreds, very likely thousands, of other persons will receive from our efforts. The great majority of these persons are not known to us during the time of our effort and most of them will not yet have been born. We simply will not be around long enough to receive the degree of benefit from our labors that will come to many who as children will begin their Christian life in the buildings we erect.

Building committees must do all that they do unselfishly because the building is theirs only after it is first for the Lord and others. What they do will have consequences down through the years long after they are gone from the scene. This is why personal prejudices or sentiment or lack of knowledge or any other limitation must not be allowed to color the judgment of the building committee member. He is under the holy obligation to decide everything unselfishly according to one principle: What will serve the Lord and His people best now and tomorrow?

The moment the congregation is satisfied that it has described exactly what it wants to do in its new or improved building, it is ready for the architectural service. All sections of the building committee that have been studying and writing the program are now dismissed, their work finished. A small building committee now carries on into the architectural phase.

The building committee must carefully select its architect. The architect they choose will need to be a man who understands what the written program says. He needs to be a man who, in addition to his professional competence, is capable of identifying himself sympathetically with the faith and the work of the church. The building committee's work with the architect is chiefly that of an interpreter of the congregation's life and task. This underscores the importance of spelling out the day-to-day work schedule of the church for the architect.

The problem of actual design is not the committee's business; it is the architect's. What the building is to say is largely up to those who are the members of the church; this has been expressed in writing. The architectural expression is up to the architect.

Although building committees must say what the church wants and why, they should never dictate the architectural forms by which these requirements are to be met. If the witness of the building is to be understood, it must be addressed to our time and to the community in which it stands. The architect should know how to accomplish this better than anyone on the committee. But architect and committee must work together for vital expression. They must recognize that many of the old symbols of architectural and artistic expression which characterized our buildings in the past have lost their power for today.

The architect, then, if he is to be true to his profession, must with the church try as best he can to speak to the passer-by in terms that are alive with the brisk shapes and the symbols and materials of construction which are available to us in our generation. We need to give our architect some liberty in using his medium as his religious expression.

A church will be wise to avoid any prolonged debate about the relative merits of traditional or contemporary style. On this limited plane nothing can be resolved. Let us at least rejoice in the fact that architects today, when faced with the problem of designing a church building, do not sit down to study the blueprints of churches built in the twelfth and eighteenth centuries.

Rather than engage in a wrangle about styles, let both the church and the architect strive to erect a building which is surely and decisively expressive of the Word of God in the life of this American decade. We should be concerned simply that the building bears eloquent outward witness and have inner functional adequacy.

"Oh, yes, this is all very well, but the true Christian can find God in any situation," some may say. But most of us find our religious faith through tangible and outward means and events in specific times and places. For us the proportions and design of the church building, its beauty as well as its holiness, are instruments which make the unseen near and real. The building is not the whole story, yet when it is coupled with a congregation whose people are faithful, it does become a place where to most persons the glory of God and His presence is felt.

All the efforts of the committees and the architect to witness will be seriously handicapped if our buildings do not have their origin in the deep sense that the Church is the Body of Christ ministering to a needy world.

Martin Luther once said, "Anyone who is to find Christ must first find the Church. For how can one know where Christ is, and where faith in Him is, unless he knows where His believers are? Whoever wishes to know something about Christ must not trust to himself, nor by the help of his own reason build a bridge of his own to heaven, but must go to the Church, must visit it and make inquiry. Now the Church is not wood and stone, but the company of people who believe in Christ; one must keep company with them, and see how they believe and teach and live." [3]

It has been characteristic of the great ages of church architecture that they rose out of a vital faith. We would do well, then, in our day, to think through our deepest religious convictions and to give them fitting expression in an architecture which makes these convictions intelligible and inviting.

A well-planned, beautifully designed church edifice bears effective witness to that unseen spiritual house not built with hands, of which Christ Himself is the chief cornerstone.

[3] Quoted in Luther D. Reed, *The Lutheran Liturgy* (Philadelphia, 1947), frontispiece.

3

BUILDING FOR THE CHRISTIAN COMMUNITY

The following was the opening address delivered at the Annual National Conference on Church Architecture, Los Angeles, California, February 17-20, 1959, jointly sponsored by The Church Architectural Guild of America and the Department of Church Building and Architecture, National Council of Churches. The address was first published in Your Church, *April-May-June, 1959.*

Building For the Christian Community

As first speaker at this conference, I am eager to say something about the conference itself. This conference does not begin today. It is one of a continuing series that originated in its present form about nine years ago, growing out of regular smaller public meetings of churchmen and architects going back another ten years or so.

Over this span of time, two exciting realities have emerged.

1. A really broad scale ecumenical enterprise which I believe is unequaled, or certainly not excelled, in what it attempts to do, in any other cooperative Protestant activity.
2. The emergence of a group of professional men — the architects and craftsmen of the Church Architectural Guild of America who give more and more of their time at their own expense to work with thirty or forty church denominational executives in the church building field affiliated with the National Council of Churches' Department of Church Building and Architecture.

What is happening here in Los Angeles this week is firmly rooted in long preparation, country-wide and local. We like to think that each conference is better than the one before in that the persons attending go away with a clearer understanding of *all* that is involved in a building program. Each year, less time and effort are squandered in attempting to answer individual questions that are mainly architectural with more time spent on fundamental things which are of far more value to building committees than information concerning architectural ad hoc details.

I think it is well to make it clear at the outset that the purpose of these days together is not to give off-the-cuff, architectural curbstone service, but to give guidance in the basics of building-program planning and to point out where and how you can find help to do it.

Now, having said this, we are where we want to be. Building for the Christian community is a religious task, primarily a task of practical theology which must begin with the consideration of many other things before architecture. It must begin with the insides and the deep down verities of the Christian community.

Let us look for a moment at this unique entity we are calling the Christian Community. We might just as well have said "church" but the word has been with us so long and has accumulated so many extraneous meanings that it no longer announces its particularity. If we do not know the church in the full punch of its particularity, we cannot build for it significantly.

The Christian community, the church, was born at Pentecost. But the church was conceived on the eve of the first Good Friday. Our Lord Jesus Christ sat in that famous upper room with a group of men just like ourselves, men with mixed backgrounds, capabilities, and views on all the issues of life, social, personal, religious. One man was at such variance with the others that he had already determined to wreck the fellowship by betraying its leader to His powerful enemies.

What happened there that evening, all those who name the name of Christ in faith have been celebrating ever since. So holy and intimate a thing it is that only the initiated truly participate. What happened? I like to think of it in a way that to my mind ties it in with everything that is important to the on-going life of the Church and that defines "church."

Our Lord told that little group of men who were like ourselves that he was going to leave them. He would be delivered up by evil men and crucified. They would have to carry on His mission. In one way, the accustomed way, He was not to be with them any longer; but in another way, a sacramental way, He would be with them more certainly than ever before. "Here is some bread," he said, "think of this as my Body which is broken for you." And then, "here, take this wine, think of it as my Blood, the very essence of my life, which is shed for you and for many for the forgiveness of sins." It is as if He said, "These elements are the real signs of my continuing presence with you and of grace and power. I will be the center of your lives and you will be my body, my hands and feet to do my work in the world. When I come to you in the Holy Spirit, greater work than I have done, you will do." And, "As the Father has sent me, even so send I you."

One definition of the church would certainly be that it is the community, the fellowship of those who remember Jesus Christ and carry on his work. When one thinks of what happened there in the upper room, and then later on Pentecost, one immediately sees that the church is more than this. It is, indeed, what the New Testament has called it, the Body of Christ. It is much more than an organization. It is an organism. It is a peculiar unity with a life within itself which of itself it did not create.

Where do we begin to build for such a community whose existence is centered in Him who, Peter said, is the "Pioneer of life"? If we are to build significantly for such a community, function and structure must be rooted in this unique and divine event. To partly quote Dr. Joseph Sittler,[1] we must begin with the statement, " 'The Word became flesh and dwelt among us.' This statement puts us at the central place for pondering what the form of a Christian church should announce. 'The Word' is Christ. He is the concretion of what God is, demands, and gives . . . 'The Word became flesh' means that this reality, this saying, this requirement, and this gift has occurred in history where we live. The Christian faith is not a bowing of men before a dream of religion. It is not a mission that is simply moral. It is the adoration of men before the gracious act of God's Christ, given and alive within man's history house. 'And dwelt among us' means that this new reality is alive here and now. This dwelling creates a community that responds to it, that lives by the fact of it, calls itself the very 'Body of Christ' in the body of this world."

The church does not exist for its own sake. It is a community with a mission. Its business is to glorify God's Name and do His will; to train its members in Christian faith and character; to proclaim the love, the law of Christ in the gospel, to the whole world and thus to turn men to Him and to serve His kingdom.

[1] *Architectural Record* (Dec., 1955), pp. 190-1.

This is the nature of the Christian community as it is believed and confessed, so far as I know, by every member denomination of the National Council of Churches of Christ. This being the nature of the Christian community, it is apparent that the empirical church (the church as we know it) has drifted far from its moorings in the Christian event. This makes the business of building for it very, very critical today.

Social analysts tell us that though the church as we have described it is still alive, it is definitely no longer informing or shaping our American culture. This now is not the least of the church's problems as it builds in the midst of the world's communities and seeks to carry out its mission. It must be concerned not only about the shape of its own special community but the natural, secular community of which it is a part.

An especially penetrating analysis of the religious community in America today was offered to the readers of *The Christian Century* in a series of articles last fall by associate editor Martin E. Marty.[2] He pointed out that once "Multi-faced Protestantism had a virtual monopoly in *forming* the religious aspect of American culture and went beyond religion to inform the culture as a whole." The Protestant command of the religious situation "has been displaced by religion-in-general, that is, by a temporalized national religion" lacking in nearly every respect the dynamic particulars of the New Testament concept of the church, the Christian community, which we have described.

As the fruit of American pluralism and nationalism, a *fourth* "religious community" has developed in the national scene. It is clearly in the ascendancy and cer-

[2] Martin E. Marty, "The New Shape of American Religion," *The Christian Century* (Sept. 10, 1958), p. 1019.

tainly in the majority, though unorganized. It has no clear label. It is what the American is who is not definitely a Protestant, Roman Catholic, or Jew. This fourth community is a curious amalgamation of many religious instincts and positions diluted to fit a rationalized secular humanism. "God is a chummy partner, the 'man upstairs' . . . Fellowship with the Lord provides an extra, emotional jag, brings happiness and personal success. Be kind to other people in order to be happy. Love God and you will be a success." In this outlook, all understanding of the church as the Body of Christ has disappeared. The Christian community as the continuum of the reality and the mission of the gospel, as the God-centered nexus of God's grace and man's response in thanksgiving, service, and obedience is simply not in the picture.

"Protestantism must decide whether it believes God can be packaged or not, whether He is subject to man's manipulations or not. At the very least, Protestants must measure the distance between present positions and the original ones, must note the extent of erosion. And such reference to what was, places upon the Christians of the reformation alive in these post-protestant, post-Calvinistic times responsibility for reintroducing the prophetic note. At present, someone else is calling the signals; longing for the good old days avails little." [3]

You see, we have come to a kind of impasse in the march of our faith. We cannot afford to be vague as we confront the natural communities of our time. What we really believe about God and man meeting in Christ must be given first place in our building programs. "Every effort to give our Christian tradition palpable declaratory force must be set forth, point to, hold up

[3] *Ibid.*

and draw to the single Christ center the multitudinous details of worship. What should be celebrated in both architecture and liturgy is not general religiousness, unspecified spirituality, or a miasmic if potent mood of sheer otherness." [4] This, in its deepest dimension, is the significance of the building program. How do we build to encompass these concerns in our buildings?

First, we need to know what we believe and get it into our program so that our buildings will house meaningful activities and announce them clearly. The first question in a building program that we have got to ask and answer is, "What do we believe about God and why has He called us together in this place to do His work?" This is where we begin; not with architecture or finance, but with what we believe about God and our reasonable response to Him. Buildings for the use of the church are not ends in themselves; they are tools in the hands of the congregation for the work of the Lord. Their plan and design must be reasoned in terms of the task they are to accomplish.

Only the congregation that knows what it believes will be able to furnish the architect with the kind of data that will enable him to design creatively for the Christian community. The congregation must think and it must pray. Vague ideas about the church and its Lord will not produce an honest seeker, a thoughtful witness, or a good building. The program of the church whose people will not think under God takes on bit by bit the mores of the secular groups that surround it bidding for attention — badges and buttons, banners, bingo, and bake sales . . . and a theology without particularity, witless and anemic, with no power to save.

[4] *Architectural Record, op. cit.*

At all costs, we must avoid thoughtlessness in our building planning. Nowhere is thoughtlessness more apparent than in architecture. Thousands of our church buildings in America today are not up to housing a vigorous Christian community. It is less and less possible for anachronistic architecture to penetrate the inner life of contemporary man.

Anything can happen, and does, in the buildings that are built where belief is faltering or little or no time is taken to state it lucidly in the program analysis of the congregation. We have seen church interiors that make it perfectly clear in their confusion that the man who made the floor plan, and the building committee that accepted it, had no idea of precisely what is to transpire in a church service. I have seen altar paintings that are at variance with the Gospel. I have seen chancels where the national flag and the so-called Christian flag so dominated the altar that the sanctuary resembled nothing so much as a patriotic shine. I have seen church interiors so arranged that one would think the most important thing that was to go on there was the choir concert. Our field experience has shown that poor worship practices invariably accompany poor architecture. More often than not, the first step in restoring decency and order in corporate worship is to correct an interior fault in structure, floor plan, or decor which originated in the first place because of thoughtlessness.

Every area and purpose of the building must receive attention always in reference to what is believed. I have shuddered at the realization of how many thousands of our children, at their most tender and sensitive years of impression, are introduced to Jesus Christ and His church in moldy, poorly lighted, badly ventilated, overcrowded basements. Even we adults form our first and most stubborn judgments from the appearances and the feelings of our environment. The kind of church architecture that develops from thoughtless programing has a way of compounding our confusion about unseen realities quite unequaled by anything else in our environment. A congregation that builds without thinking through the theological implications of what it does is in grave danger of slurring the Christian event and so doing a disservice to the Lord and His people. At the very least, a building that will not in its fullest sense be God's building will result from thoughtlessness.

I regret to say that I have visited many buildings in which the kitchen is the best planned room and the most adequate and best equipped for its function of any in the whole building complex. What can one believe about this other than that the congregation understands better what goes on in the kitchen than what is meant to happen in the sanctuary or in the classroom?

The primary task in church and church-related building is to see to it that what we believe gets said in what we build. Failures such as we have been describing stand the best chance of being avoided by conducting thoughtful program studies with the results carefully written out and communicated to the architect at the time he is commissioned.

The second condition that must be met if we are to build adequately for the Christian community is to properly divide the tasks of the building committees and the architect. Architecture is the business of the architect; the description of the church's life and purpose, what it believes and what it proposes to do about it is the business of the congregation. Much must be done by the congregation's committees before drawings are made or any construction is begun. Building committees often start at the wrong end of their task; they begin busily with the problems of architecture: What will the building look like? Where will it be placed on the site? How much will it cost? It is a waste of time to try to answer questions such as these at the beginning of the building program and, indeed, to try to answer them at any time without the assistance of the architect and until they have written a description of all the activities that they intend to promote in their community.

One of the happiest trends in recent years is the slow but steady increase in the understanding of these matters. The people of the church are having a larger and larger share in contributing to the character of their building. I don't mean by this that they are designing their buildings; but they are increasingly able to express to the designing architect what it is they want their buildings to do and say in the community which they are to serve. This is happening because more and more persons involved in building programs are giving attention to first things first. They realize that before a meaningful structure can be designed, everything that is believed and what is needed to address the community must be communicated to the architect.

The congregation's work of describing the life and task of the church and the archtitect's work of planning the building to house it calls for carefully thought-out procedures of administration and timing. This requires knowledge that most congregations do not have but which is easily learned. A letter of inquiry to the Department of Church Building and Architecture of the National Council of Churches will bring an immediate, helpful response. A brochure with detailed directions as to how to proceed in a building program will be sent to the inquirer. Most major denominations have building departments, departments of church architecture, and related agencies who will also furnish competent guidance in the organization and management of building programs.

The moment the congregation is satisfied that it has described exactly what it wants to do in its new or improved building, and has written this out in clear language, it is ready for the architectural service. A small building committee now carries on into the architectural phase of the building program.

The selection of the architect should be made on the basis of objective consideration of what he is to do. He needs to be a man who understands what the written program says. He needs to be a man who, in addition to possessing professional competence, is capable of sympathetically identifying himself with the faith and the task of the church so as to design fittingly for its witness and work. He, too, will think before he acts, inspired by the congregation's and the committee's thoughtful program analysis.

The building committee must know where its competence ends and, after it has written its program, carry on with the architect in the role not of critic but of interpreter of program intentions. The architect's business is to put the program into three dimensions. Out of a clear understanding of this division of labor is developing today a new rapport between the church and the architect and it is a new thing though once, centuries ago, it was the common condition. Here is a development of fundamental importance in all that we try to do in conferences of this kind and to each of you who face the problem of providing building facilities for the work of the church. One finds expressions of it today in architectural magazines. In *Architectural Record,* June 1958, there is an excellent expression of it. It is a quote in an editorial from an address by architect William Caudill to the Wisconsin Chapter of the American Institute of Architects.[5] He said, "We had better make more effort to find out what our clients need, not necessarily what they want. There is a difference — a big difference. The salesman capitalizes on wants; the truly professional architect concerns himself with his client's *needs.* The analysis of these needs is today the most important phase of architectural practice." Mr. Caudill called it also the weakest part of today's architectural practice though he noted that there were indications of progress by a few practitioners. "These days we are hearing more about *programing.* I'm not sure that's the right word for us to use. It reeks too much of the mere listing of space needs. What I'm talking about is more than listing. It's really writing specifications for an architecture in terms of a qualitative space as well as quantitative space."

He insisted that architects must learn to determine the problem as well as to solve it. "Architectural practice is destined for activities which will require less drawing and more thinking . . . The skillful and creative designer as always will remain the key man in the architectural process because a great architecture results from the fusion of creativity with the skill of architectural composition and the technical knowledge of the day."

I have deliberately until this moment said nothing about style. I have done this because in building for

[5] William Caudill, "Wanted: Architectural Diagnosis," *Architectural Record* (June, 1958), p. 9.

the Christian community style is a result, not a starting point. It is most depressing to reflect how many building committees begin their programs with consideration of style. What is more depressing is that they are sometimes misled in this way by architects who are more willing to please their clients than to truly serve them.

When it is once understood that style has little or nothing to do with the essence of architecture in the service of the church — that it is only the result of many other things that must come first and that it is primarily the architect's business because it is in his competence and not the committee's, it will be recognized that any discussion of it in a congregational meeting can be little more than an opportunity for the voluble to air their prejudices. If we are committed to the communication of the Gospel to the communities in which we witness, we have no choice but to see to it that our buildings are designed to speak to average men and women who know little more (many less) about the Christian event than they know about nuclear physics. Together we must seek and find those physical and psychological factors by which we may speak in terms that are vibrant with the brisk shapes and new symbols of this hour.

Our buildings will not speak to the community unless we know whereof we speak. Let's face it. There will be better architecture for the church, an architecture able adequately to carry the burden of the church's task as a tool and a symbol, when there are better Christians.

We will not have succeeded in building for the Christian community if when the building is erected, our use of it is uncertain or inarticulate. The liturgical acts in the sanctuary, the church school and fellowship activities, all must be performed in accordance with a positive conviction in, and expression of, the Christian event. The congregation's behavior must not mask what we believe and what we say happens in church.

We blunder too often in this respect — result: our buildings stammer.

I am reasonably certain that for seasoned Christians it may not be at all necessary to make so much of church architecture, may not even be necessary to have a special building facility. If the church had no responsibility to either the immature Christian or the non-Christian, probably any kind of building would satisfy our private needs for our closed community. But the church building is not a private expression only, something whispered within the family circle; it is a public matter. The building and what we do in it and with it confronts the whole community.

Member and non-member alike must be led by what he sees in church where building and people are one to glorify God and to feel there that he is at the gate of Heaven.

In addressing the cultural community architecturally, the temptation to win quick but shallow response with jazzy decorative details and odd shapes must be resisted. Architectural expression is so much a community matter that for the church it must enclose its eloquent spaces with a dignity consonant with what the church is and what it has to say.

Now then, in summary, building for the Christian community means simply a thoroughly reasoned approach by the churches to all building problems based on our best knowledge of God's act in Christ in our behalf.

To do this successfully involves:

1. Knowing what we believe and seeing to it that it gets into our building so that, both as symbols and tools, our buildings serve the Lord and the task of His church.
2. Seeing to it that building committees and architects know and properly divide their tasks and then perform them under the disciplines of faith and logic.
3. Realistically appraising the current religious situation (its own community) and the nature of the natural community which the church must address; always remembering that when we build, it is to celebrate the Christian event and to provide a building in which and through which, under the guidance of the Holy Spirit, the church, the body of Christ, performs its incomparable mission.

4

THE GLORY FOR WHICH WE BUILD

The following was originally an informal address delivered intimately to a small group of architects and clergymen gathered together in retreat fashion at Princeton, New Jersey, in the summer of 1959. The meeting was sponsored by The Church Architectural Guild of America and the Department of Church Building and Architecture, National Council of Churches. This paper was published in two parts in Your Church *in the issues of April-May-June, and October-November-December, 1962.*

The Glory For Which We Build

"I will praise the name of God with a song: and will magnify him with thanksgiving." Psalm 69:30

THE PURPOSE of this paper is twofold. First, to name the elements in public Christian worship that occur universally in every age and culture where the Gospel is proclaimed and to which men respond corporately *in church;* and, second, to offer some observations regarding our common task in architecture and the allied arts to shape the building environment for the support of the congregation in its corporate acts of worship.

Apparently at no time in our century until quite recently has the design for worship among Protestants been based upon program considerations as we understand them in our circle. Space has been designed for worship without a previous understanding of the act of worship itself. That this error could continue over so long a period of time without being more apparent is due to the fact that the image of the church building inherited from the past has long been an integral part of the landscape. Almost no one questioned its adequacy as either a tool or a symbol for the church in a changing world.

The spiritual pressures of our day are pushing for

answers to questions regarding the nature of the Church and her mission. It is now widely understood that an adequate architecture for public worship must begin with a knowledge of the nature of worship.

However, it is not enough for the architect or the church building counselor simply to discover and appreciate Christian worship as a concept isolated from its expression and activity by an assembled body of worshippers. Worship understood as a dogmatic, psychological or philosophical concept is not the thing for which we are designing when we shape and decorate the house of worship. Concepts of worship are interior personal phenomena and vary considerably from person to person.

The analysis of worship that would be most relevant and fruitful for the architect would be that which deals with worship as an activity rather than as an idea or mental image. While it is certainly necessary to know what individual members of the church with a building program believe about worship, it is much more necessary to know what they do about it together *in church.* It is worship as a corporate activity which the design is to take into account primarily.

I would like to insert here that I use the terms *public worship* and *corporate worship* interchangeably, I believe, rightly. I am not attributing to corporate worship any mystical quality that it may or may not possess. I mean by the term simply people worshiping as a body, but each worshiping as an individual, which is the only worship possible. Nevertheless, they worship as persons linked together in a common action in orderly patterns. A body, an assembly of individuals together in one place at one time with one over-arching purpose, requires an architectural setting in many ways radically different from that required by an individual alone, that is, apart from others physically engaging in private worship.

I think it is not possible to design for worship as a concept because it cannot be precisely enough defined for architectural expression. Dr. Luther Reed says in his new book that while certain elements of the experience of worship "may be mentioned . . . their deepest values vanish under analysis, even as the loveliness of a flower is lost when we pick it to pieces." [1] Our task is not to build for these "elements" of worship abstractly, but as they are publicly expressed by the assembly of worshippers in visible, audible, concrete acts *in church.*

Every tradition in Christian worship, high church and low, announces five basic elements that come to light in the worship of the Church. Dr. Joseph Sittler's analysis of the elements of worship is extremely relevant. [2] He calls them Recollection, Thanksgiving, Participation, Proclamation, and Expectation. You will note that these are all words of action finding expression in movement, speech, song, and ceremony. The Christian Event to which they point and celebrate here and now is the glory for which we build.

God's act for men sets going responsive acts in those who hear and see. *In Church,* these responsive acts are felt inwardly individually and expressed outwardly collectively in public worship. The worshippers remember the mighty acts of God in their behalf. They remember that they are in this place at worship and that what is happening is something that happened first from God's

[1] Luther D. Reed, *Worship* (Philadelphia, 1959), p. 1.

[2] Joseph Sittler, The Shape of the Church's Response in Worship (A paper delivered at the North American Conference on Faith and Order, Oberlin, Ohio, Sept., 1957).

side. "What is announced is one and continuous with what has been announced since the Resurrection." [3]

Recollection engenders thanksgiving which is expressed by the congregation in acts of praise, prayer, repentance, dedication, offering, etc. By and through Word and Sacrament, the congregation *participates* in the Christian Event. They recognize themselves as truly members of the Body of Christ. They are new creatures in Christ.

There is a growing understanding of these things in our time. The Church is recognized as an organism rather than an organization. It is not an institution among institutions; it is indeed the Body of Christ. Thus it is holy and unique, unlike anything else on earth. It is a distinctive community with a mission. One does not join church; one is called into it by the Holy Spirit; born into it in baptism. The Church, understood in this New Testament perspective, is the underlying reality of public worship.

I am sure some of us recall that a year ago Dr. Homrighausen and Dr. Dowey of the Seminary here at Princeton reviewed some of the concrete results of liturgical studies surrounding the doctrines of the Church and the ministry. I review these briefly: The sermon is of a piece with the whole service and is of no greater or lesser importance than anything else that is done in church; the centrality of the Word and the Sacraments; the Church as the body of believers gathered about the Word and the Sacraments; the minister not speaking *at* people but *with* them; the church is not run by the preacher but the church is a community with a pastor; all together, pastor and people, become a worshipping community.

[3] *Ibid.*

Always as participation Christian worship is inevitably *proclamation.* As we participate we proclaim to each other and to the world the truth God has let us see in Christ. "Every service of public worship is a banner of life flying among the banners of mortality . . . The celebration of the Lord's Supper is indeed recollection and it is the seal of the forgiveness of sins and the gift, and the nurturing of life in the Lord of the feast. But it is something more; something immediate and poignant in the embattled 'little flocks' of the first century, known again in our day by millions in shattered and cut-off lives in cells, rubble, behind wires and iron curtains. It is a proclamation of this special recollection which is the Church, of engrafted membership in a kingdom not born of history and, therefore, not at the mercy of history's demonic tyrannies. The somber chalice has in our day again become a definite sign uplifted, the believers' toast of terrible joy." [4]

As often as you eat this bread and drink this cup,
you proclaim the Lord's death until He comes.

One note that is missing from the interior architecture of our buildings is the spirit of triumph and everlasting victory. Here is something we can all work at. It is far better to spend time thinking about how the "Church Militant" can proclaim its triumphant faith than to worry about many of the things that we do.

The proclamation of the gospel remains the Church's primary business. The Church's worship and her mission belong together. For this proclamation, language is the chief medium. The vital acts of worship are framed in language which illuminates them and makes them intelligible. We use, of course, not only words but other media, visual and aural. Here is the major,

[4] *Ibid.*

perhaps only completely good, reason for building the best building possible. Expectation is the last of the five elements found in full Christian worship. Though it is the last in the order of our discussion, it is no less important or significant than the other elements and is interwoven with all of them. In recollection, for example, it is because of what was that what is and will be is expected. St. Paul said, II Cor. 3:4-9: "We dare to say such things because of the confidence we have in God through Christ, and not because we are confident of our own powers."

The strange and wonderful thing is that even though we are still in this life with its sorrows and all its limitations, at the same time we expect victory and the life beyond. We already in fact possess it in Christ.

It is hardly necessary to say in this group that we cannot deceive ourselves and believe for a moment that the churches we serve and the committees we deal with have a clear picture of these things. Worship as a weekly function of the congregation, and, as a primary use of the building, is understood superficially but not fundamentally. Millions of church members go to church without the faintest notion of these things we have been thinking about. The mystical nature of the church itself and its meaning in the world is not understood any better. I regret to say most architects are no better informed than their church clients about what really happens in church.

But there is something on the credit side in our business. At long last, Protestant churches are finding out that Sunday worship is very much more than a weekly gathering of pious people and are realizing, often with quite a jolt, that it is not enough to go into a building program with a handful of statistics, a fundraising campaign, and an architect. The awareness of this is growing apace everywhere in the country and among all the denominations. My great concern as an administrator and presumably an authority in the field of church building is that the movement does not outrun our preparation to be of service. It is just possible that while we are trying to shift gears, the movement may bound ahead in characteristic American exuberance with a new thing and soon be without reason or direction. My concern also is that our Department of Church Building and Architecture of the National Council of Churches and our brothers of the Church Architectural Guild of America are alert, know what is happening and have answers and ideas. Our task of informing the churches is never-ending. This growing change from romanticism to realism in building for worship is the finest thing I can remember having happened in my day in this field. Of course, it means more work for us but it will make us better men and will build better churches.

If the liturgy is considered not merely as a fixed form of worship but as the dynamic expression of people in the worship of God, an expression which involves the presence of God and the response of the people, then it follows that a building for worship should provide a setting that will serve every corporate experience of the congregation in the action of the liturgy.

An almost overwhelming temptation for all of us, but especially for the architect, is the desire to design for emotional effect, art for art's sake, at the expense of liturgical usefulness and significance. Our designing must be under the discipline of the liturgy. The liturgical function of the church building must be the principal criterion in evaluating ecclesiastical architecture. James F. White had this to say:

> The provision which is made for public worship is the special concern of the theological criticism of a church building. This category, by far the most important in evaluating churches, is the most frequently overlooked. As a result, it is in this area that our churches have their greatest deficiencies.[5]

Designing for form and effect without full concern for substance and liturgical intent is sheer charlatanism. The "atmosphere" which we want our church interiors to have is not achieved by artistic contrivance. What we want is given rather than achieved. It appears in the finished building as a result of having successfully captured in design, insofar as this is possible, the meaning and action of public worship. Because of the liturgical awakening that is occurring in all the churches, the day is almost upon us when nearly any average guy will be able to spot a spurious "religious atmosphere," one that is contrived rather than inspired. An "inspired effect" so far as it can be described by natural terms results from an obvious harmony among the many formal and decorative elements that are proper to liturgical expression.

Design, to be successful in the sense we promote, must fix its attention upon the liturgical realities and not be enamoured of calculated, contrived emotional effects. How, in a setting in which the primary and immediate emotional effect is that of awe or peace or mystery, is one to be specifically confronted in the company of his fellow worshippers by the living Word. The prevailing effect of the environment must be one with the elements of Christian worship which we

[5] James F. White, "Church Architecture: Some Standards," *The Christian Century* (Feb. 18, 1959), pp. 196 *ff*.

enumerated and thus stimulate their richest expression. The failure of so many church interiors to match the awakening need for an environment that will lovingly embrace the activity of public worship is our long-standing failure to differentiate between private and public worship; i.e., individual and corporate worship.

There is, to quote Professor James F. White, ". . . danger that in concentrating on the emotional aspects of the building, we focus our attention too exclusively on the building's function in private worship." That is, an individual may think of the surroundings quite apart from their function as a place for public worship. "Private devotion is subjective and individual, frequently involving considerable feeling and emotion and often quite inarticulate. One's surroundings can play a very large role in promoting private worship; but without at all disparaging private worship, it can be said that the confusion between it and public worship is the greatest weakness of contemporary Protestant worship. Most of our services zigzag between elements of private devotion (silent meditation, solos, etc.) and elements of public worship (confession of faith, hymns of praise, etc.). Certainly we must encourage the use of our churches for private devotions and the emotional factors which contribute to them must be carefully considered. But let us not forget that the primary function of the church building is to be the facility for public worship." [6]

Cardinal Lercaro, in an address given at the opening of the First National Congress of Sacred Architecture in Bologna, Italy, September 23, 1955, underscored the liturgical function of the room of worship. The cardinal said that there have been times in the

[6] *Ibid.*

history of liturgical architecture when the function of public worship has not always remained unimpaired by design. Yet so faithful has the Church been to the principle that even in cases such as the omission of the apse by the Jesuits in their churches of the sixteenth and seventeenth centuries, there is good reason. In this particular case, the reason was that the Jesuits emphasized the active life, and counterbalanced this emphasis by the practice of mental prayer which is eminently individualistic. "Thus the choir was suppressed because it was the expression of the monastic spirituality, which is eminently communal."

I believe it is not possible to overstress the importance of keeping always before us, as we go about our task, the distinction between private and public worship. If our work, as it must, is to advance the growing understanding of the Church among us and deepen the participation of our fellowmen in the life of the church, it is evident that the crucial criteria for our architecture are liturgical rather than individualistic or, shall we say, conventional.

This particular confusion about worship has plagued us and plagues us still. At its door can be laid so many of the errors in the plan and decoration of our church interiors.

If we do not keep the distinction between an individual person at worship and a congregation at worship, we cannot counsel or design adequately for worship. While an educated taste and a desire not to be dated may prevent us from recommiting many of the old errors such as putting the choir stalls front and center and by various tricks of design exalting the preacher and the deacon, without this criterion we will not escape making new blunders. I see new abominations in the making, the direct result of architectural exhibitionism with its egocentric rather than theocentric motivations.

A present menace to the liturgical spirit is the nationalistic, moralistic, homogenized religion of America. This is one of the not so hidden persuasions of our time and has an influence that touches us all in one way or another. This demonic spirit knows nothing of the Church as the Body of Christ and cannot, therefore, wherever it is influential, have anything but damaging effect upon an adequate architecture for the church. Of course, other factors in the social complex of our times impose hurdles that we must learn to leap or circumvent in some way if we are to pursue a rational and liturgically inspired architecture for worship. Among these factors is the great drift toward standardization in materials and techniques so apparent today in the prefabricated church package deal.

To return for just a moment to the point that it is necessary to remember that we design for public worship above everything else when we design the church building: it must simultaneously be kept in mind that the interior architecture must also provide for a variety of non-liturgical devotional functions. Indeed, I feel that perhaps the crowning test of a really successful interior would be that it serves as well for the person who comes in from the street to pray apart from his fellows as for the assembled congregation in the principal liturgical service. It is not as difficult, I think, for a small church to do this as it is for a large one. Perhaps the crucial consideration in all of this is the right disposition of the free and furnished spaces of the floor plan and most especially the disposition of the liturgical centers.

I am indebted to Edward Sövik, a Lutheran architect of Northfield, Minnesota, for an insight regarding the architect as a "liturgical artist." He said, among other fascinating things, in an address in Minneapolis in April, 1959, to a specialized group similar to ours here today, "The usual criteria of architecture are not adequate for the design of a church. Vitruvius, for example, is not our man. For the liturgical artist, an additional criterion must be added to Vitruvius' 'commodity, firmness, and delight.'" The criterion Mr. Sövik believes should be added is, in a word, *significance.* The house of the church should at once announce its significance as the place of assembly for the people of God. It is clearly a community gathered about faith for participation in the Body of Christ for the proclamation of the Word and the celebration of the Sacraments.

This criterion and those derived from the liturgical spirit should consciously dominate our evaluation of our work and that of others in building for public worship. I think all of our accustomed criteria, and certainly our prejudices, should be periodically examined. During the past year in several regional conferences and in some semi-private sessions with congregational committees, I have pleaded for the attitude as promising the most of everything in the whole building experience from program writing to dedication day as one of complete open-mindedness. I suggest the best way to begin a building program for both congregation and architect is not to start from where they are, but to examine critically everything they believe and start back of it from absolute scratch as if no one in the world ever built a church before.

I refuse to think that no new form is possible, that the last line has been drawn for an architecture suitable

8

CHRIST CHAPEL
EPISCOPAL ACADEMY
Overbrook, Pennsylvania

Vincent G. King, A.I.A.
Architect

ST. PAUL'S LUTHERAN CHURCH Mount Prospect, Illinois

Stade, Dolan, Anderson & Bonesz, Architects

10

THE UNITED CHURCH
Rowayton, Connecticut

Joseph Salerno, A.I.A., Architect

11

12

13

THE BAPTISTRY, CHURCH OF THE SACRED HEART, Audincourt, France

Maurice Novarina, Architect

14

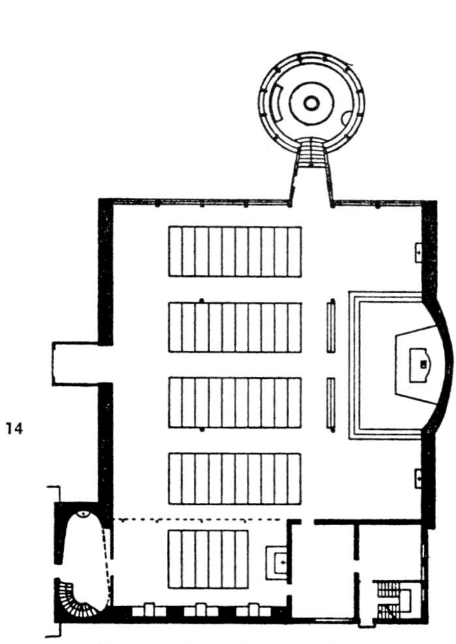

ST. MARIA KONIGIN CHURCH
Cologne, Germany

Dominikus Bohm, Architect

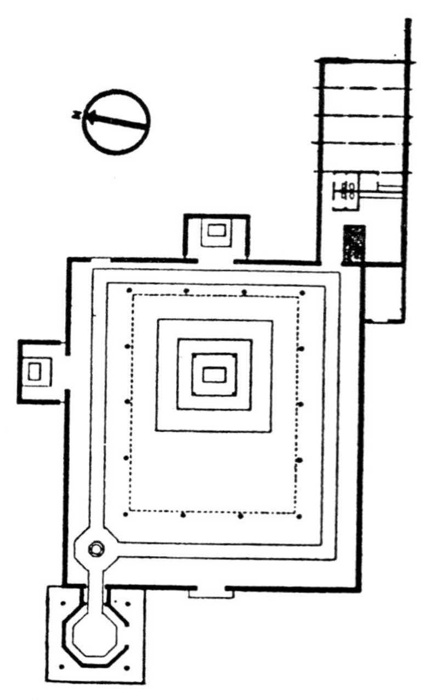

15

ST. PAUL'S CHURCH (Anglican)
Bow Common, London

Maguire & Murray, Architects

for public worship. I am certain that we are not at the end of the road. For the same reasons, I am equally certain that there is no single floor plan that is perfectly appropriate in its location of every element that is to be preferred above all others in every situation for all liturgical actions.

All formal patterns of worship and most free, informal patterns that I have observed begin with some declaration that is intended to set forth the fact that all that is about to happen is in God's name. The so-called "Trinitarian Invocation" is the common beginning of the historic liturgies — "In the name of the Father and of the Son and of the Holy Ghost." This is the deliberate recollection that God is present and that all that is to follow in the service happens because of what God has first caused to happen in Christ.

Immediately, it seems to me, this fact, which is the matrix of the liturgy, should set the pace for the architectural design and decor. The architecture should announce that this is God's house, that what happens here is His initially and then ours by virtue of the fact that He has called us and has received us. H. Grady Davis has said: "Christian worship . . . is our answer to God in Christ, an answer awakened to the moving of God's spirit inside us. Not men calling and God replying, but God calling and man replying!" [7]

There are many ways in which the architecture can say, "In the name of the Father and of the Son and of the Holy Ghost." Whichever way is chosen, in order to succeed, the foci of the room must be clear — the fact of God's presence among His people.

Over-decoration, clutter, and pinched areas are the

[7] H. Grady Davis, "Theological Foundations of Christian Worship and the Arts," *Response* (Pentecost, 1959), p. 4.

common enemies of dignity and order in the church room. Altar, font, and pulpit must be visible and stand apart from other furnishings. It is probably best to have these symbolic and utilitarian pieces free standing. But, wherever they are located and however they are designed, the basic requirements are an abundance of free space around them and subdued and non-competitive backgrounds. Any decoration of the pieces themselves must be appropriate symbolically and executed in such a way as not to obscure their meaning, form, or use. In short, everything must have theological significance. Purely aesthetic reasons for any arrangement, design or decoration are not sufficient for the church.

Providing free spaces in the nave in connection with the seating of the congregation is of much significance. Though many disagree completely with him, it is profitable to think of what H. A. Reinhold has to say:

> Liturgically speaking, fixed pews are a nuisance; they turn the church into lecture hall or auditorium. They not only immobilize the congregation physically to a high degree, but they bring in a psychological element of immobilization and regimentation. The congregation becomes an audience, spectators. The celebrating throngs are gone; the informality so much needed to create ease and enthusiasm, the grouping of families, are made almost impossible. Lightweight stools, rubber pad kneelers for the average, sitting benches for the old and infirm along the walls, ought to be the answer. (I have no illusions that this will ever come to pass.) [8]

The liturgical revival in our time has bred dissatisfaction with the typical basilican, rectangular floor plan that is the long established inheritance of the western

[8] H. A. Reinhold, *Speaking of Liturgical Architecture* (South Bend, 1952), p. 18.

church. I think the dissatisfaction is due not so much to the rectangular form as such as it is to its unintelligent, habitual handling and the clutter that invariably ensues when for budget reasons the areas must be reduced without a corresponding reduction in the furnishings and program intentions. Moreover, it is distressing to note in many churches of recent vintage which use contemporary structural elements and materials, the floor plan with all the flaws that have accumulated in the last hundred and fifty years is unchanged. The architect has looked forward to the extent that artistically speaking the building can be described as contemporary but the congregation itself has looked backward or nowhere at all.

The Gothic proportions of the rectangular plan of one-third chancel and two-thirds nave, rigidly adhered to, do not in my opinion serve the liturgical purposes as they are informed today by the liturgical renaissance. Insisting upon such proportions, as I know some counselors to do, does not result in a floor plan that supports the liturgical elements we examined at the beginning of this paper. For example, there is a falling off of congregational participation beyond the fourteenth pew. Even in a church seating as few as 250 persons, especially when a choir of thirty or more is placed antiphonally in the chancel, the "west" third of the rectangle in the nave is not as functional as the middle third or "east" half of the nave. The rear area becomes the haunt of those who are not really of a mind to be much involved in the liturgical actions that stem from the chancel area.

Additional reasons for the reexamination of the typical long rectangular church have been advanced. They are certainly worth noting. In the familiar ground plan, the chancel-sanctuary complex is very much differentiated from the nave. The Church is one community, not two. Should there not be one space instead of two? Should not the clergy, choir, and people be one body together in one space, its limits defined by the normal ranges of sight and sound? Edward Sövik asks the question, "Don't we do better with our symbolism if we suggest God among us, working in and with us as our Lord suggests? The presence of God is not more real up front on the other side of the communion rail." This disturbs me. The depth of some chancels is so great with the altar or the table so remote from the nave that the doctrine of the universal priesthood of believers and the universal elements of participation and proclamation are architecturally denied. Half of the people at least are so far away from the visual and spiritual foci of the room that they can hardly think of themselves as more than mere observers and listeners.

The most decisive thing we need to remember in church (this is the element of recollection) is that God in Chirst is with us. Mr. Sövik suggests that a solution is to frankly design so that we have several foci, each in its own right to become the center of liturgical attention in the service when its particular significance is to the fore: pulpit for proclamation; altar for thanksgiving, intercession, confession, etc. In a letter he wrote last year to a pastor with a building program in Tanganyika Territory he had this to say among many other interesting things:

> In general, however, I might say that we think we should dispense altogether with the idea of separate nave and chancel so that the activity of worship is dispersed through the space and there is not any dominating focus in the room, but a series of foci —

the prayer desk, the pulpit, the choir, the font, the communion table, and other symbols. The design should be such that the congregation is caught in the matrix of the liturgy and cannot easily think of themselves as merely an audience. This is the priesthood of all believers.

In respect to liturgy, it is important that there is flexibility, and it is also important that what activity accompanies the progress of the words of the service be such as to illuminate these words. Whatever movement there is must not be arbitrary or meaningless. This, if anything, is what is wrong with high church liturgy, that it can become, at least to those in the pew, form without content.

In order to keep observations such as these in due perspective, it must be observed, for example, that the altar, because it is a piece of deep and varied significance, would have to continue as the dominant one in the chancel. Indeed, even in the few settings that I know in which there is an unconventional arrangement with a number of liturgical centers, the altar turns out to be more pronounced than in many a chancel with the longstanding familiar arrangment. It would seem that the altar will remain the key piece and the major focus in the church room.

In Protestant planning, the altar will always have to be given a great deal of thought because it is so rich and comprehensive a symbol. Its varied symbolism which is its great strength can also be a weakness. A result of its complex association of meanings is that it is often planned to mean so many things that it is clearly anything. Thus often the most important function of the altar, namely, that it is the table of the Lord and our sacramental fellowship with Him, is weakened. The Roman church has no confusion about the altar. It is for them a place of actual sacrifice. Since this is the all important part of their rite, neither the design of the altar nor its dominent location in their churches is open to question. With Protestants, because we assign primacy to neither Word nor Sacrament and because we do not concur in the Roman concept of the mass, the situation is quite different. In suggesting a solution to this problem for the Tanganyika church, Sövik, in the letter cited above, says:

> In view of these considerations, we have concluded that it is best to make the altar a table, free standing, approachable from all sides, preferably not located so as to dominate the church continuously. It should share in importance with the pulpit and perhaps the font, each of these becoming the dominant focus when the activity of the service is centered in or around it, but not otherwise. . .

The fine arts in the service of the church must also be under the discipline of the liturgy and the liturgical spirit. There is time only for a paragraph on this subject. I quote from the Rev. Josef A. Jungman's book, *Public Worship*. Jungman is a German Jesuit. His book, translated now into English, is published by The Liturgical Press, Collegeville, Minnesota. It is a book well worth reading. After speaking of the value of the arts for the church, he writes:

> Admittedly the arts do also constitute a danger for the liturgy. The social prayer of the people, for instance, finds expression in song; next this song is refined to a higher artistic standard within the competence only of skilled singers — and the people become condemned to silence. . . . The altar which is essentially a table, is equipped with an ornamental centerpiece displaying, for example, a picture of the saint here venerated. From this centerpiece of

> Romanesque art there develops the gothic folding triptych; and from this in turn grows the colossal reredos of the baroque period, by which the essential features of the altar are disguised rather than emphasized.[9]

In our terms the result of this common sequence of events in artistic expression when sight of the liturgical criteria is lost is that the significance of the altar is lost. Consequently, it no longer plays its role as a visual aid in recollection or proclamation.

In a relatively recent development, this seems to have happened in the altar turning up as a shelf. Designers seeking novelty or economy produced a mere bracket on the "east" wall as a substitute for the holy table. Whatever the reason for this, it was at the expense of significance.

We continue the quote from Josef A. Jungman's book, *Public Worship:*

> In art, there seems to be a kind of centrifugal force, a tendency to break loose from the holy foundation of humble divine worship and to become an end in itself. It is necessary, therefore, constantly to return to the living principles for its proper use. . . . And we should not find it a matter for unmixed regret that the prevailing poverty of these days has necessitated the choice of simple forms in church building and ornamentation, since through these the essential basic thoughts are more easily expressed and can be more easily understood.[10]

Just as there are certain universal characteristics that distinguish Christian corporate worship wherever it is found, so it seems to me, there are certain universal characteristics of successful church architecture. A

[9] Joseph A. Jungman, S. J., *Public Worship* (Collegeville, 1957), p. 6.
[10] *Ibid.,* p. 7.

paper I wrote a few years ago attempts in its last pages to name these characteristics. We wrote that a proper building for public worship will be theologically correct, ecclesiastically proper, and characteristically true of the One we worship:

Theologically correct:

Architecturally speaking, this means that every object that meets the eye must belong to the high purpose of the room. The room must possess unity and all objects, decoration, and arrangements must be such as to preserve that unity. The architecture must emphasize the action of the liturgy. This must be so because the liturgy of the church is the expression of its faith celebrated in the corporate worship of the congregation.

The building must possess strength and beauty in a form appropriate to its peculiar task — a witness, a proclamation, to member and non-member alike of the honor in which He is held by the congregation which erects this building to His Glory and as a sign of His continuing presence with His people. The building would not be theologically correct if it was badly situated, poorly designed, carelessly programmed, too cheaply or too expensively built. (Better the building be incomplete but well done than be complete but of flimsy construction and makeshift design.)

Painting and sculpture should be reclaimed by the architect for their services to the church. The witnessing function of the arts can and should be more than a mere decorative function.

Ecclesiastically proper:

The building will provide a proper material and esthetic setting for the task of the congregation and its worship, so planned as to make every provision for the orderly gathering together of the people in response to the Gospel, to magnify the means of grace and to surround every liturgical action and emotion with decency, order, and beauty. Whichever of the two principal ground plans which have survived the ages is chosen, basilican or central, it can be ecclesiastically proper only if it points beyond itself and environs appropriately the whole Church, Head and members. The room must not suggest an auditorium. It is something entirely unique and this must be quite evident. The singing here is no concert; the preaching is no lecture. This is the place of divine encounter that is recollection and fervid thanksgiving, present participation and proclamation, and prayerful expectancy. The worshipper is met before One who has manifested Himself in time, the Word become flesh, who is here in His house as a Presence and not simply as an idea.

Characteristically true of the One we worship:

The building will have beauty and structural honesty and be frankly of our making. It will be of the community but also in dialectical relationship to it, pointing to a divine community above. The building's beauty will not be designed primarily as an attraction to the outsider, though it will be that in a measure, but as an offering to God.

The building should have a quality that I call "innocence" by which I mean that it must be honest and should not be self-conscious. It must not seem to over-reach itself. It must be without pomposity, declaring that it must fail as just a building, to be characteristically true of the One we worship. This quality must be thought of as in opposition to display, baroque elegance, or architectural virtuosity or exhibitionism lest the building seems an end in itself

> and thus conceals God. This means a good reason for every detail of design and no decoration for decoration's sake. It means sincerity in structure, no faking in anything. Any representational art should be of the kind that is a starting place for one's thinking and emotional response and not a stopping place, that once you have seen it, you have not seen all there is.[11]

Both architect and church-builder must be ready to seize every opportunity to speak to the truth that the church building must fail if the people who gather there are unmindful of its purpose and do not, therefore, know how to use it. No matter how near perfection the edifice is technically, how purely expressive of purpose and function, the business has not been worth it if the people who erected the building are not one in purpose with its noblest intention. It is hard to say it, especially for us and for any who give of themselves and their means sacrificially, but, the building is nothing!

What is something, and of inestimable worth, is a congregation at a time and a place made wonderful by presenting themselves and their building as living sacrifices "consecrated to Him and acceptable by Him" (Rom. 12:16). Of such a building founded on the clear call of our Lord to be His witnesses, Rudolf Schwarz wrote, in *The Church Incarnate:*

> In the great and real sense there is indeed little purpose for by ourselves we build no churches: that God must do. . .
>
> Thus the church building is an exalted song composed out of individual and congregation, out of

[11] See the chapter on "The Role of Theology in Church Building," above, pp. 22-23, 25-26.

> space, construction, and the act of worship, into all of which the same eternal measure is sunk deep . . . Where this exalted song rings out, a church has been built. . .[12]

"I will praise the Name of God with a song and will magnify him with thanksgiving." *(Psalm 69:30)*

[12] Rudolf Schwarz, *The Church Incarnate* (Chicago, 1958), p. 230.

5

WHY WHAT WE BELIEVE SHOULD DETERMINE WHAT WE BUILD

This paper was presented as an address on the occasion of the Annual National Conference on Church Architecture in Minneapolis, May, 1960, sponsored by the Church Architectural Guild and the Department of Church Building and Architecture, National Council of Churches. Its special purpose was to direct the several workshops that followed to give primary attention to those things which in the author's opinion are most essential in planning church buildings. As it is printed here, it contains a number of paragraphs that were not used in the address because of time limitations. In a somewhat different form, with editorial changes, it appeared in Protestant Church Buildings and Equipment, *September, 1960.*

Why What We Believe Should Determine What We Build

We haven't a moment to spare. Without a word of humor or welcome, I've got to start at once or I will not be able to say in the twenty-five minutes or less what I have to say to make it worth your while to listen.

It is self-evident in all of life that what we believe, really believe, absolutely conditions what we do. In the matter of planning and building for the church, it is so evident that he who runs can read.

Church building is a human problem long before it is an architectural or a financial problem. While we tend to attribute the inadequacy of so many of our edifices, even those of recent date, to obsolescence and other factors, the real failures arise from the lack of straight thinking on the part of the church at the outset of its building program. Our problem-buildings stem largely from thinking more about the structure than the reasons for building it. If our buildings are to express adequately the purpose, and implement the task of enlightened congregations, building plans must begin with beliefs about ultimate things.

If we are wrong-minded or uncertain as to what the church should say and do, then it follows, as night the day, we shall end up with the wrong kind of building. By the same token, if we are right-minded, if we take time to get our ideas of the work and worship of the church clearly conceived, our buildings will come out right.

As Christians, we believe that what God has done for us in Christ must inform us in everything the church undertakes. The act of building, the building itself, and what we do with it, and in it when it is erected, are all involved. The building program ought to begin with what we believe and proceed from there to completion under the church's highest and deepest convictions about the Christ Event. Our buildings must bristle with belief or they fail to advance the Christian witness in the midst of the smog of secularism which has settled down so rapidly over our present-day communities. So we say, "Think! before you build." Think especially about what the building is going to do for the congregation, and what the congregation should be doing in the building. Buildings are both the tools and the symbols of the church. As such, they must reflect in function and in form what we believe, or they are not worth our money or our effort.

So, when we build for the church, we do not begin with architecture or the architect. We begin with the fact of the Christ Event, the fact of the Incarnation: God coming to us in Christ once and sufficiently for all time for our salvation, His continuing presence with us in His Body, the Church. Ours is a religion of revelation and revelation is always bound to a time and a place. Here is a note of particularity. This must be first: what we believe about God and our reasonable response (Romans 12:1) to Him, which corporate and individual response our building in our time and in our place is to shelter, support, celebrate, and proclaim. We must realize that we do not only worship in our buildings, but that we also worship with them.

What we believe about God and about man under God and about God's mighty act in His Son in our behalf and our faithful response in worship, work, and obedience are the beliefs that must motivate our planning and shape our buildings. And these beliefs as we practice them in concrete acts of worship provide the basic indispensable data for the architect. But it all begins with what we believe about God's deed for us in Christ, and the nature and the business of the church, or we build in vain.

It is, as I have said, so very necessary that our buildings bristle with belief or we will not be able to advance the Christian witness in a time when it is so generally impoverished. This is the answer to the "why" of our deed. There is a difference between the Church and everything else on earth and this difference must be clearly celebrated and announced by every means that we have. We have got to get through to our time. We aren't, you know. We aren't because most of the time in moments of decision we teeter between expediency and principle.

Rational planning of buildings for the church is often stymied by the phony communications psychology of the prevailing culture which seems to strike its highest moments in emulating or sanctifying celebrities, worrying about filter feed-back, and dreaming "I was a concert pianist, or a medieval princess in a Maidenform bra."

If we do not know what we believe or if we do not believe earnestly or deeply what we believe, or if we are unable to give, in St. Paul's phrase, a reason for the faith that is in us, we cannot inform the architect or open him to inspiration. Consequently, the building cannot be a good tool or a good witness. Without right thinking, we may end up with a building which is nothing but an imitation of what may or may not have meant something of vital importance to men of another time and another place. At worst, we may get a speechless building when we need most desperately to speak to our contemporaries of the only really *good news* the world has ever had and about which the voice of our common culture is silent. A merely imitative building cannot move men to heed the witness of the church. "Costume" architecture or a contemporary building that is merely novel, won't work. The first, because it will immediately be associated with a number of obsolete symbols that claim no part in today's existence. The second, because it is only a splash on the landscape and rooted in nothing but a passing fancy.

Our times seem to say to the average man, in the church and out of it, that the vital and interesting and manly things in the world have no connection with the church. The popular image of the church is altogether askew from the New Testament concept of it. Robert W. Spike, who spoke at the Los Angeles conference last year, writing in *The Christian Century,*[1] in describing a screen play that seemed to him to depict the role that many people think the church played in American life, said, ". . . a kind of religion that occupies a perpetual high spot on the nostalgia Hit-Parade. Religion stands for the dear, dead past that is nice to keep enshrined and occasionally touch for luck. It stands for being a Good Boy or a Good Girl." What of us

[1] Robert W. Spike, "No Holy Charade," *The Christian Century* (Jan. 6, 1960), pp. 11-12.

who know that this is not what we mean by religion? How do we build a building that says it isn't? How do we build to say what we do mean and advertise the ineffable act of almighty God in Christ for every man, everywhere in every time?

I am irresistably reminded of Karl Heim's passage in his great book, *Christian Faith and Natural Science*.[2] He is illuminating the same point in another area of the Christian mission, though the figure he uses is intimately architectural. "There was a time in the Western World," he said, "when the whole body of the profane sciences, especially philosophy and natural science, was merely the handmaiden of theology." He continued:

> Today the situation is changed. Amid the totally transformed environment of the modern academic discipline, the basic assumptions of which have entirely altered, if the confessions of faith of the reformers is stated at all nowadays, it makes the same impression as would a last remaining venerable fragment of wall, all that is left standing of a medieval cathedral in a half-destroyed town appearing as a foreign body amidst the newly erected blocks of offices and flats of a modern city.
>
> During the last war, a deep impression was made when, after an air raid on Mayence, all that remained standing of a church dedicated to St. John the Baptist was the fragment of a doorway on which were inscribed the words: "Repent ye: for the kingdom of heaven is at hand!" But this ruin from the past could not be left standing like that permanently. Either it could be built up again into a complete church of a design which fitted in with it, or it would have to be pulled down and cleared away. In a present-day university, with its research institutions and clin-

[2] Carl Heim, *Christian Faith and Natural Science* (New York, 1957), p. 27.

> ics, the theology of the Reformation makes a similar impression. Either this ruin from the past must be cleared away — that is to say there is no room left for theology in a present-day university — or else this fragment left over from another section of reality must be built up again and completed so that it forms a comprehensive world-picture. Unless this is done, it has become meaningless.
>
> Only when the whole is again visible, of which this fragment is a part, will it be possible to discuss it seriously. But the question here is not the relatively unimportant one of the position of theology in the structure of the present day university. Something far more important is at stake; namely, the credibility of the Christian message in the world of today.

Well, this is the kind of world in which we are called to build for the church. This is the practically boundless dimension of our task. I would say there can be no evocative, eloquent, communicative church building without a congregation that knows what it believes and knows what it wants to do in today's world about what it believes, and then finds an architect, who may not be the cheapest or the most expensive, but who comprehends the true dimensions of the problem and can go as far with it as architecturally possible.

The creation and use of church buildings has become a necessary part of our work and witness and must, therefore, rest on the same premises as everything else we do in response to God's call in Christ.

The architecture that will do most to help the church break the cultural barrier is the architecture that will provide the most intelligent solutions to the creation of proper space for the activities of the congregation.

Now these general ideas and admonitions and the one directive, *to think,* should furnish a proper background to your workshop discussions. I would judge that workshop group a failure that would behave as most building committees do; that is, start with architectural considerations and work backward to program. What happens, of course, is that usually the church never really gets to the program. What the building is going to look like and what it is going to cost are in the full focus of attention so that a nebulous but nevertheless vital thing, a program, is lost sight of as being of primary importance, and is given only secondary consideration.

True architecture like good religion begins with putting first things first. I hope the workshop that is listed "Organizing to Build" will give much attention to the respective roles of the congregation, its committees, its leaders, its counselors, and that they will be defined and sharply contrasted with the roles of the architect, the artist, and the contractor.

There are many kinds of building program procedures but all good ones have in common the placing of program decisions first in order of attention and the consideration of architectural design and finances following. All good schemes will carefully divide the role of the committee from the role of the architect. Program is the business of the congregation; architecture is the business of the architect. In my opinion, this workshop group would do exceedingly well if it spent much time in considering ways and means of communicating with the architect. More and more I am convinced that this area may well be the most critical one in the cooperative work of committee and architect.

The way to make a thing significant is to make it

precise. A precise program must be written by the church that leaves no act of worship or teaching or fellowship or service undescribed. The failure or the inability of a building committee to transmit a precise statement of what it believes about its faith and its task has a definite effect upon the resulting design. The architect will attempt to fill the vacuum thus created by designing for emotion rather than faith and work or doctrinal meaning.

I would earnestly hope that the workshop groups "Building for Worship" and "Christian Education" do not forget, but take into full account, what they believe about worship and parish education. There are penetrating new ideas and some old ones we discovered we have got to use in our planning and designing because they are better answers to man's need today in this time of confusion than many thoughtless ways of doing that persist among us.

Never in the history of the Church has so much concentrated attention on so wide a front been given to assessing our ways of worship and teaching. The meaning of the Church and its holy task has taken on a new relevance. We need to be aware of these things and order our thinking in the light of them.

Full of meat for the building committees and the architects is the article, "Religious Education and the Design of Protestant Churches," by J. Gordon Chamberlin.[3] (This article has been reprinted from *Architectural Record* and is made available from the Department of Church Building and Architecture of the National Council of Churches.) I quote one paragraph from the article:

[3] Gordon Chamberlin, "Religious Education and the Design of Protestant Churches," *Architectural Record* (Dec., 1959), p. 152.

> There is a deeper and more significant way in which the education program has been accepted as part of the life of the Protestant church. The change of attitudes comes from both sides — educators and the churches. Sunday schools no longer feel they have done their full jobs by telling children about the Bible and by developing individual character. To be a Christian means to be a part of the acting Christian Family, the church. The education task is carried on because it is part of the church's mission, and conversely it is part of the educator's task to introduce children and young people into the total life of the Christian Church. Christianity is the faith of a community, of the people of God, and the participation of children in the Sunday school is their way of participating in the life of the whole Christian Church.

The workshop on "Building for Christian Education" must weigh just such considerations as these. It is a matter of great concern to those of us who are charged with the responsibility of counseling the congregations of our churches in building that, for the most part, they seem to be content to build without taking thought, just as though the ways of teaching today need to be no different from what they were before the First World War. We see plans of parish education units come to our office for review that one would swear were copied line by line from the floor plans of buildings built fifty years ago before any of the rich findings about teaching-learning relationships, that we now have, were known. Tiny rooms and miniature chapel and auditorium arrangements are apparent in which the child or young person has no role but to sit still and listen.

I have seen too many church school rooms badly

built and decorated, utterly inadequate for any kind of thoughtful program with an impact. For example, I have seen cramped rooms with "toy altars" in them. From the evidence at hand, the altars were used for little more than a catch-all spare table. I have found comic books tossed on them, pickle jars with punched lids for pennies, and, once, an old cigar butt.

The whole program of Christian education must be weighed carefully in advance and the purposes of the building studied before any architectural planning is begun. Until this is done, no man on earth can design appropriate space for the educational activities. The appointments and decoration of the church school rooms are to be considered as matters of the greatest importance. These problems and the architectural solutions to them that have been tried and that are in the making should occupy the major part of the discussion of the workshop on "Building for Christian Education."

The workshop on "Building for Worship" has its work cut out for it in the same way. We have been building churches for years as if they were auditoriums with the preacher and the choir as a kind of permanent cast addressing the passive people in the pews. This is a sadly mistaken concept of worship. It has led to some of the weirdest behaviour in church history as well as to poor doctrine and surrender to the blandishments of secularism.

No way of worship that divides the Body of Christ in what is essentially a corporate act can be right. The understanding of the church and the ministry that has come strongly to the front today right out of biblical and historical research sees the people, pastor and choir as one together before God, all doing essentially the same thing together in worship. The pastor is not someone apart from the congregation; in the part he plays, he is simply "the chief worshipper." The sermon is no more important than any other part of the service.

Here are expressions of the New Testament principle of the universal priesthood of all Christian believers. Why this doctrine and the Protestant doctrine of the ministry so central to Protestantism, have had so little effect on the form of the church building has always puzzled me. We see floor plan after floor plan for new church buildings that are virtually medieval in their concept and arrangement. The building is so long in proportion to its width, and the depth of some chancels is so great, that the altar or the table is so remote from the greater part of the nave, that the doctrine of the universal priesthood of believers is architecturally denied and half the people are so far from the liturgical foci of the room that they can hardly think of themselves as more than mere observers and listeners.

Many new churches are rising, however, in which this problem and others are being met. Considerable experimentation, sparked by liturgical studies, has been going on in recent years and almost everywhere new churches are showing the results of sound thinking about worship. Naves are becoming shorter and wider, the holy table is coming nearer to the people (even radically central plans are being built; i.e., ground plans in circular and polygonal forms with the high altar in or near the very center of the whole composition), choirs are disappearing from the chancels with the result that chancels are becoming less cluttered and hence more useful for the purposes for which they are chiefly designed. Altars are being set out from the "east wall" and made free-standing. This enables the communion rail to be on three or four sides of the altar or holy table, thus accommodating many more communicants at one time and heightening the corporate sense of participation in the church's most distinctive act of worship. Fonts are being placed in such chancels as these and accented architecturally with altar and pulpit as, in my judgment, they should be. In such cases, the lectern is often eliminated and the lections are read from the altar.

What happens in church is the criterion to be taken into account first, last, and always in designing churches. The workshop on "Building for Worship" should discuss ways and means of communicating to the architect the congregation's understanding of worship and its meaning and, very necessarily, what they propose to do about this understanding; e.g., what part music is to play in the service, how they are to commune, etc. It would be well to list all corporate activities that are to take place in the room and describe them. It is necessary that these matters be settled first before there is any talk of architecture as architecture, furniture or equipment or the use of the fine arts. As a matter of fact, there can be no intelligent discussion about the material aspects of the building until the elements of its function and specific purposes are settled. One works in a vacuum otherwise. Building committees almost invariably make the error of talking about architecture much too soon, before they know what they need, just as they often ask, "How much will it cost?" before they know what it is they are going to buy. I am simply arguing that answers can have meaning only if the questions do; solutions have reality only as they are related to specifically stated problems.

What will be the appearance of the building? That

is an unavoidable and important question. But it must be asked at the proper time. And the time to ask it is *not* at the beginning of the building program. It can be asked with meaning only when the functional elements of the building are fully known; i.e., precisely what is going to take place within its walls. The whole approach to the problem of design is cluttered with pitfalls. A faithful pastor and a good friend of mine wrote to me some months ago saying that the old congregation he is presently serving will probably have to relocate because his building is obsolete and the plot is much too small. He requested a picture or photograph of a fine contemporary church building, preferably in color, that he might hang up to stimulate the people's thinking about the new church building. I wrote him in part as follows:

> I honor your idea of hanging a picture. It may do some little good but I am afraid that it can't mean much. What stimulation may come from it is short-lived and superficial at best. We usually counsel the avoidance of this approach. Our reasons are:
>
> 1. There is usually a chance of deception. The church building you need and ought to have may not remotely resemble any picture used for promotion.
> 2. Using pictures puts the accent on the wrong place. It accents form and appearance rather than significance. You don't really want to have a new building for its own sake. You want a new building to do better work in your community. The use of pictures, especially at the beginning of a building program, accents architecture and not the task of the church. At the beginning it must be program; i.e., the meaning and purpose of all the activities in which the congregation engages

> to make a glowing witness. The people must think of purpose, mission, the advance of their work in the Lord, and then when all this is settled, face the architectural problem.
>
> Even at this later stage, attention to architecture should not become the congregation's chief concern. Rather, its chief concern should be training in the most effective use of the revised program that will be made possible by the anticipated new building facilities.

The designing of the building will have to be consonant with its purpose. Buildings for the church must match thought for thought, purpose for purpose, goal for goal. With these intentions, belief will determine the stance of the structure in the community. It is a kind of creed in concrete for which I am pleading, but without the static overtones such a phrase might suggest. Rather, I am thinking of the living, working sweep of such forms as Nervi has created which, though they are in rigid concrete, transcend all static suggestion. I am thinking of an ecclesiastical architecture addressed to our time as well as to God which will be as different from traditional expressions as, say, J. B. Phillips' paraphrase of the New Testament is different from the King James Version or even the revised Standard Version of the New Testament.

I do not know whether beauty can consciously be built as beauty into a building or anything else. I suspect not. I don't think we know what beauty is precisely enough to create it consciously. I think beauty is something that is given. I think it is a quality that invests the artifact after the artist has done all that he can do to make it right according to concept and function. I think, too, it is as much in the eyes of the beholder as it is in the object itself. I quote from the Easter, 1960 issue of the publication *Good Work:*

> It is no news that most automobile bodies are designed for the maker rather than the owner. This $3,100 1960 model, with its 6 tail lights and similar extravagances, is styled to satisfy the illusions of prestige built up by advertising. Beauty does not result from this effort, but rather from adjustment of realities, such as structure and function.

It seems to me that we have a word of warning here to architects as well as to those building committees that will insist on playing architect.

I must take a moment to say one more thing that I believe the workshop group on "Building for Worship" should discuss because I believe it lies at the heart of the problem of adequate design for worship. I see so much of what I call aimless design, especially in churches that have had a large budget, the kind of thing which when it is in church seems to be art for art's sake alone. My associate, John Whetstone, in reference to the interior design of the church room and its furnishings wisely prefers the phrase, "facilities for worship," rather than the expression, "the setting for worship," which I have been accustomed to using. I think he is right; the latter phrase has an overtone that belongs more to the theatre than to the sanctuary. The true significance of the furnishing and decor of the liturgical centers lies not in what we *feel* emotionally, sentimentally, about them when we see them, but in what we *make* of them and what they cause us to reflect upon in the full context of corporate worship, the degree of clarity, in fact, that these objects possess as sacred symbols rather than as exciting works of art.

Except the architecture and the furnishings call to

worship, they are not proper for the church. Many situations are indeed "a setting" and as such they fail to be a facility for worship; there is a strong secular connotation, a glamor focusing attention upon itself, easily obtrusive and smacking of stuff and nonsense. I see too much attractive design frankly contrived for sensual effect, demanding attention by strong visual impact and delight, but unable to deliver any meaning beyond itself, once it has captured the eye. The visitor says of it, "Yes, beautiful," or "Very clever." He is excited or calm, or pleased depending upon his temperament; but, he is not edified, nor is he brought to his knees by any vision beyond the moody execution of the object or setting itself.

I am disturbed by the increasing number of attempts I see to design and furnish buildings without reference to liturgical or doctrinal significance. Some months ago, I contemplated a very rich interior done manifestly as a "setting" for worship. Visual delight was everywhere, but theological or liturgical significance was hard to find. This is a condition that arises quite spontaneously out of insufficient thought and vague commitment. Sacred symbols, while beautiful in design, were for the most part used illiterately or ungrammatically. Latin crosses abounded ad nauseam; they were even used as door-lights. The baptismal font could be found only by searching and, when finally it appeared, it seemed to be more an element of artistry than of meaning. Such design is merely scenery. The trouble with it in church is that it exists at the expense of meaning where meaning must be nearly everything.

The effort to make beautiful the furnishing or fabric of the building without giving first thought to, or announcing, its liturgical meaning or doctrinal significance will not result in ecclesiastically proper design.

This is an important work we do these days. I want to quote a few fine words from Ernest Koenker's wonderful little book, *Worship in Word and Sacrament:*

> From the involvement of their own personal lives and from a world of recurring tensions, not a few people are saying today: "Lead us to a real and living God. We have known enough of what life under our own resources offers, convince us of God, and we will gladly surrender ourselves to him." It requires a layman or pastor who himself has struggled under God's law, with the dark night of doubt, irrelevance, and despair and who has come out victorious to point the way through his proclamation of the gospel. But the church has for centuries employed its public worship with just such a missionary approach . . . (in the Holy Communion) . . . Here God gives Himself in the sacramental elements of the service and man acknowledges his indebtedness to God in the sacrificial. This is no theatrical invention, based on clever psychological insights. Here man is led into the presence of God, Who took the initiative once in the redemptive work of Christ and is active here again in His means of grace.[4]

The building program is a part of the Lord's work. See how important it is that we think and pray in the doing of it. I have come full circle. Whenever I contemplate the act of thinking and prayer, I am reminded of the old archbishop's remark in Bruce Marshall's story, *Satan and Cardinal Campbell.* Said the old bishop, "Two things can save the world, thought and prayer; but the trouble is the people who think don't pray, and the people who pray don't think."

[4] Ernest B. Koenker, *Worship in Word and Sacrament* (St. Louis, 1959), pp. 67-8.

6

ESSENTIALS OF GOOD PLANNING FOR CHURCH BUILDING

At the Delaware Valley Conference on Church Architecture, Building and the Arts, sponsored by the American Society for Church Architecture, at Grace Presbyterian Church, Jenkintown, Pennsylvania, March 1, 1962, this was the keynote address. It was published in The Journal of the American Society for Church Architecture, *No. 2, April 1962.*

Essentials of Good Planning For Church Building

ONE THING I must make clear at the outset. It may not be necessary in this gathering, but I'm not going to take the chance of disappointing anyone. I am hardly going to say anything about architecture and the allied arts as such! Reason: architecture, good architecture, for the church is the result, *not* the starting point for a successful building program; and I am speaking of the building committees' role in church planning, not the architect's. I am making two assumptions that I always make in addresses of this kind or it is a waste of my time and yours for me to speak. The first assumption is that most of you are here because you are engaged in a building program, or are about to be. The second assumption is that most of you need to know more than anything else the true nature of what it is you are doing, or are about to do, when you plan for church building and the role you must play as committed persons in the building enterprise.

There are many essentials to good planning for church building but the one absolute essential is the building committee's understanding and proper execution of its task. All the many other essentials to good planning are relative to this one. I have nearly always believed this and time after time in my ten years of serving congregations in building programming, its truth has been confirmed by brutal facts.

In every church building program failure that I remember the one constant factor has been the building committee's failure to see its proper role. Those of you who have had any experience at all in this field know precisely what I mean. There seems to be no instinct for reasonable building planning. Perhaps it is only because they have so little knowledge of what is involved that building committees almost invariably begin at the wrong end of their task. They begin busily with the problems of architecture — What will the building look like? How big will it be? What will it be made out of? Building committees that begin their work with these questions can have no idea of their essential task in planning. Building committees must do a great many other things which are their essential business and then depend very heavily upon an architect who knows his business before it is reasonable to ask such questions as these and before there is any hope whatever for good answers. When the building committee knows just this it can do its job with a high probability of success.

Every crucial element in essential planning pivots upon the building committee's vision of its task and upon its competence. This premise is confirmed every day in my work. This past summer, it was confirmed in another and, to me, unexpected way. I read from a report I made to my department following a European study tour of church buildings:

> I don't believe any of the outstanding church buildings we saw could have been built by a typical

American building committee with its often captive architect . . .

Our new churches on the whole lack the ecclesiastical and architectural distinction we found in most of the European church buildings. Pondering this phenomenon, I was driven to the conclusion that these buildings are what they are principally because they are *not* planned and designed by building committees of the American mold but by knowledgeable clerics and creative architects chosen for the most part by competition.

Apparently the job is done in an atmosphere free from short range views of economy and the sentimental restraints that limit us in design and the use of materials. The result is that manifest thought and skill are lavished on the fabric of the buildings to the shunning of ornament for ornament's sake or its use to disguise poor materials and shoddy, careless design . . .

(We had conversations with a good many of the churchmen and architects responsible for the achievement we saw.) Hearing them speak, it was not difficult to explain the eloquence and distinction of their buildings. One discovered in these men a degree of knowledge and conviction about the church and its mission that is not common among even the clergy in our land. . .

The men and the buildings they are building or are causing to be built are of a piece. Theirs are the same frustrations common to all creative work in any society but their efforts are not short-circuited by building committees as often as in our work. . .

. . . that approach to church planning and design that properly divides the task between the committee and the architect, with both parties informed by a more than casual knowledge of the mission of the church in the world, was confirmed (as the road to success). . .

Now I want no one under the impression when I am finished this morning that I have argued for a conversion of our committee system. I do not mean that at all. Nor do I mean to lament the committee system. There are values in it that I would not for a moment want us to be without. There are byproducts of tremendous value to the church, equal to and exceeding the architectural results. I have often said that if all that resulted from a building program is a good building, no matter how excellent, that program is a failure. For a building program to be a success, not only must a good building result but a new congregation, new in its understanding of its life and mission in the community where God has planted it. Nothing offers a congregation so great an opportunity for a new life of work and witness as a building program properly conceived and executed. If all the research and study, responsibility and decision is placed in the hands of a small group of experts, though a good, perhaps great, building will emerge, the people are untouched and a great opportunity for the congregation to grow in grace and understanding is lost. I am for the committee system but, if it is to work, the building committee must know its business.

The useful, communicative expression of anything, be it a sermon or a building, must start with a consideration of the meaning and purpose of that which is to be given expression. Some knowledge, as much as it is possible to have, of the meaning and the goals of church building is essential, as well as ways and means of involving the congregation in depth in the enterprise. Church building is a human problem long before it is an architectural or financial problem. It is essential that the problem be stated *by* the congregation rather than *for* it by someone else. The people must know what it is they really do when they build. And they must know precisely why they are building. The first essential step in good planning under the committee system is to involve as many persons as possible in a study of the church and its mission. They write out the results of their findings and what they mean to do about them. This is the program and this is given architectural expression by the architect.

It is as important to know what is *not* essential to the committee's business as to know what is. For example, it is not really essential that in writing the program the committee give to the architect the exact number of square feet or a hundred and one similar things of architectural relevance. If the architect is the right architect, he will know or can find out easily enough the size of the space needed and the way to heat it and light it and decorate it. The one thing that must be given to him by the committee, the one thing he must know positively that he cannot find out elsewhere, which must come from the committee and can only come from the committee, is a full description of the activity that is to be housed in a particular area and the kind of persons, and their numbers, who are to be engaged in it. This is the committee's essential task!

There are a good many of us here who, while we are not on building committees, have occasion to consult with them in one way or another. I am in this group and I have a critical word to say to fellows like us. I think it will illustrate a point I am trying to make about as well as anything I can say.

Anxious to be of help, we often come to building committees with ready-made counsels about architectural matters. We do not face the committees or the congregation with their real business, with the result that building committees are not clear as to what it is they must do and why. They miss consequently the great thing, the great essential, which is knowledge of how their role differs from the architect's.

We are so ready to speak of solutions before the committee has seen the problem in depth or sometimes before they have seen it at all. We unwittingly become conspirators with them in their natural disposition to play architect with all our quick talk about standards in space requirements, building materials, budgets, floor plans, color schemes, heating systems and all those things which commonly crowd our consultations and conferences about church building.

Talking so much about such things and so little about the congregation's part in building is to neglect the weightier matters. We succomb to the temptation to put packaged solutions before building committees and somehow there is always the atmosphere of haste and pressure which is inimical to creative, thoughtful and prayerful processes. We must examine ourselves in this matter and not behave as if the people were not to do some thinking for themselves and as if the Holy Spirit has no place in the building program.

We act as if we had a choice and we don't; the thing is too important to override with our expertise. The congregation has got to understand what it does when it builds or it will be helpless to use the finished building properly and it will fumble all the opportunities to grow in grace and strength in this enterprise unless it tests every one of its present practices before going into dialogue with its architect. They are not helped to do this if the denominational consultant or some other fellow comes along bearing a ready-made program or architectural solutions to be warped into their situation because it is the easy thing to do or because he is so sure he is right. There is no substitute for hard work on the congregation's part. The consultant, be he the denominational expert or the architect, must guide the congregational committees, not coddle them.

I hear an awful lot of talk about the dreadful things that building committees do and I have contributed my share to it in my time, but I have heard very little talk that is realistic about what can be done to help building committees in their essential task.

Some of us here were recently at a very interesting meeting sponsored by the Department of Church Building and Architecture in the Interchurch Center in New York. Architects, artists, sculptors, craftsmen and church builders were there discussing the role of art in religious buildings. There was a good deal said about the dilemma of the artist and the building committee. A knowledgeable person said education is what is needed and said she believed some art appreciation courses for men in training for the ministry would do some good. It would. But I'm here to say that in the rough and tumble of a building program managed by a building committee that doesn't know its business, courses in art appreciation are of about as much use as a penknife in a stone quarry.

I suggest that it is far more important for the church committeeman and the pastor to know the business of the church than it is for him to know art and architecture.

No building committee has the time to play architect if it is going to do the first essential task which is to discover what the congregation believes about God and His Church and to describe accurately the corporate activities for which building facilities are needed. Later, it is essential that the responsible subcommittees be able to do certain other things such as to determine how much the congregation can afford to spend, how it is going to raise the money, etc., but these are other matters entirely. It is too bad one cannot say everything in one speech that ought to be said.

It is not possible to speak of the essential orientation of the planning that must be done without speaking of specific tasks and procedures by which this orientation is realized. Good management is certainly essential to good planning. One finds it missing so often. There should always be an agenda for meetings of the committee and the subcommittees. It should always be known in advance what the next step is and in what direction it is leading. A necessary part of good management is good timing. Discussions leading to important decisions should not begin until the groundwork laid by the studies is completed. An orderly procession of steps must be maintained. In a planned sequence, for instance, one should not go to step four from step two until step three is completed. At no time should the leadership of the program out-distance the congregation, run too far ahead. The congregation must be made to feel that it is in it.

There are immaterial as well as material goals. Because of the use which shapes our buildings and which is their purpose, it is essential in planning to remember that we do not build for ourselves and that, therefore, our decisions must not be selfishly made.

A building program is an act of practical theology.

It is not something subsidiary to or outside the mainstream of the church's work which is to thank, honor, and obey God. It is a real part of the work of making the gospel known; it is as big as the whole congregation, demanding as much thought, prayer, Christian stewardship as anything the Church of Jesus Christ is called to do. It is a matter of essential concern that building committees think of themselves as serving in this context. I am afraid they do not often do so. Usually the building program is not thought of as an opportunity to witness to the Glory of God among His people in a very definite way over a long period of time, but as something of a headache, a costly interruption in the life of the congregation and, as such, is relegated to a committee of earnest but uninformed persons who are devoted do-it-yourself fans dominated by an overwhelming compulsion to save a dime.

It is absolutely essential to know that architecture like every other human expression is first of all a matter of the spirit, the orientation of the mind and the heart and the will of people. There can be no good decision, no appropriate planning without the problem being recognized for what it is, a religious responsibility, and approached on this level of insight.

Even good functional planning for the church is still a relatively scarce thing; although it is vastly improved in this generation, that level of understanding and commitment has still not been reached which must prevail before we will see church buildings that will perform at maximum efficiency.

I don't want to talk any more about this. It is being given full consideration — a glance at the program of any conference of this kind that I have ever attended demonstrates it. I really believe we know all we need to know about how to make the church building a good tool. It remains only to apply this knowledge once we have a clear picture of program and can describe it to the architect.

What I want to spend the rest of my time doing this morning is to raise a question of supreme importance, the building as a symbol of meaning and communication. This is not only a matter of its exterior form and mass but also of the effect of its interior spaces upon member and stranger alike.

Well, let's get to it. It is the church's business to proclaim the Gospel. It does this in a number of ways. The substance of this proclamation must be the same to the outsider as it is to the church member. There is one Lord, one faith, one baptism. There must be a clear and sustained witness to the gospel. If there is not, the church will perish and deserves to perish. There is always an urgent need of lively symbols in order that men whose cultural and social environment is constantly changing may hear and see what the church is saying. The building program, not only in its method, but also in its product, plays a leading role in the eternal business of communication. This is the radical importance of external acts and images. The world judges the church as it judges everything else, by concrete results discovered in its life and practice. What the church says verbally can never be anymore than half its witness at most; what it does, is its most effective communication . . . What it does is what men see — this is the importance of visual communication — hence every visual entity must be planned to say what the church is and what it does.

Now we are not communicating too well. The old images and symbols that so long carried the weight of the church's witness no longer do so. The common faith that holds the field is what Dr. Martin Marty has described as "religion in general" . . . and it is a far cry from this to the gospel.

All that I have been trying to say about church building as a religious act and the absolute essential in good planning being a committee leadership that knows its business, comes to a focus right here. Everything that is done in the planning must be done with the idea of communication in mind.

If you accept this premise as an essential of good planning, you see that to effect it the men who do the planning and the architect who does the designing must know what it is that is to be communicated. I am comforted by the belief that a great many ordinary people in our churches know the gospel but one cannot rely on ordinary church members in this extraordinary enterprise to be creative in church programming and building.

The persons charged with the responsibility of planning must be persons aware of many things not ordinarily found in our familiar routines in the church and the marketplace. A great host of customary practices and ideas must be abandoned in order that inspired buildings might be created for an inspired communication. The men on the committee must be our best men, who hear God's living word and keep it in honest hearts, men sensitive to the human comedy and who hear "the still, sad music of humanity," men of insight who see beyond the moment and beneath it, beneath the surface of things. They should be unselfish men and men of poetic discernment.

You will recognize these things I am saying as being in a somewhat different category from essentials of organization and management and procedures. They are very difficult to capture in words but they are really the quintessential things.

I shall try one illustration by which I hope to illuminate this whole matter of the importance of the building program and the completed building in aiding the church's witness. As an outward sign of the inward truth and faith of the church, the church building is an instrument of communication. If it is to communicate truthfully, it must in no way resemble this sheet of newsprint I hold in my hand which is also an instrument of communication.

Here is the church news page of a weekly newspaper that is distributed free of charge to a good many thousand doorsteps in a cluster of suburban communities not a great many miles from here. I read a page like this and I wonder what it says about the church to the world. Let me go over this quickly. There is a lead article with a photograph showing a pastor in clerical garb with an open book in his left hand from which he is reading, apparently in the act of "blessing" a stained glass window which he is half facing.

The first sentence of the accompanying article is a dusey:

> _____ _____ – Unique impressions will be provided today during the worship services in _____________ Lutheran Church (address) when 12 stained glass windows in the church will be dedicated by the Rev. ________ ___________, pastor.

"Unique impressions will be provided today during the worship services" . . . What on earth does this mean? A stranger to the church would wonder what happens during the worship services. The label under the picture reads "_______ _______ pastor is shown in the act of blessing the stained glass window" . . . One reads this Saturday night and wonders whether it happened on last Sunday or this Saturday but then realizes that the paper is dated this Sunday so the picture is actually a phony. As a matter of fact it didn't happen the way the picture shows it. Later on in the article after naming all the windows and all the people who were memorialized, this sentence occurs, "These windows, masterfully portraying the unifying characteristics of the Christ, are the products of the studios of ______ ________ of ________." Pray, tell me what are the "unifying characteristics of the Christ"? These windows are nothing but twelve scenes of biblical events which are told infinitely better in Matthew, Mark, Luke and John than they are by these stereotyped windows that are as typical a piece of pastiche art as you will find anywhere.

Now I see two other pictures on the page. One of them is of four men wearing derbies and false mustaches and funny neckties and coats who are entertaining, "giving out with a song" as it says. Of course, whether it is going to be or was, there is no way of telling. The third picture on the page shows the same four men in the background and in the foreground four women with high hats and trick costumes that reveal a good bit of eight shapely, if oversized, legs. These four women are identified as "The Tuxedo Girls, a song and dance quartet, performing during 'A Night at Muldoon's' presented by the Rosary Society and the Holy Name Society of ________ __________ Church."

The articles on the page have the following captions:

"Joint Meeting to Conclude Center's 10th Anniversary"

"Church Societies Presented Lively Gay 90's Show"

"Memorial Mass Held for Father Washington"

"Public Invited to See Film on Water Company"

"Rev. L. J. ________ to Preach Week's Revival Crusade"

"Plans for PTA's Saturday Dance Running Smoothly"

Turning the page, one encounters a bit more of the same thing. It is a little better but generally the same trivial stuff that the church members themselves must know is inconsequential. How much of our architecture is like this!

One gets the clear impression that the church's life is one of superficial activity and confusion and that practically all the time is being spent holding socials of one kind or another and memorializing people. One reads quickly over these pages and feels like saying, "O Boy, all this and television too!" There is nothing on the first, and practically nothing on the second page that sounds one note of ultimate concern about the plight of man or his immortal soul or the mission of the church.

Ironically there is an advertisement on the second page placed by a mortician. It shows the symbol of their national society which is an Egyptian pyramid surrounded by a circle with a serrated edge. The text in part reads:

> Ever hour of every day we are prepared to serve your immediate needs. . .

When you think of it, where else would you put this but on the church page. The irony of it, it seems

16

ST. ANNA'S
ROMAN CATHOLIC
CHURCH

Duren, Germany

Rudolf Schwarz,
Architect

17

18

REFORMED CHURCH, Aerdenhout, Holland
Karel J. Sijmons, Architect

19

20

DUTCH REFORMED CHURCH, Ysterplaat
Cape Town, South Africa

H. Sikkel, Architect

21

22

ST. PAUL'S CHURCH (Anglican)
Bow Common, London

Maguire and Murray
Architects

MARTIN LUTHER CHURCH
Zurich, Switzerland

Franz Steinbrechel,
Architect

23

to me, is that it could be effectively argued that this disguised but nevertheless unmistakable reminder of death is the most moving note of ultimate concern on these two sad pages.

All this has given us some fun but I hope that it has given us some insight too. The thing I meant to show by this discursiveness is that in planning the church building (which is the most visible and abiding expression of the community which calls itself "church"), the trivial and the ephemeral must be avoided. The tremendous opportunity to tell the world something authentic about our faith and witness must be handled on a different level than the usual church page.

I believe it is Peter Hammond who points out that Rudolph Schwarz's approach to church building is admirably summed up in two principles which are strikingly embodied in the German architect's two pre-war churches at Aachen and Leversbach:

> *First,* to start from a reality based on faith, not from one based on art, this truth or reality being of such a kind as to produce a community and an artistic achievement.
>
> *Second,* to be absolutely truthful in our artistic language by saying nothing more than we can say in our times and nothing which cannot be understood by our contemporaries.
>
> If what we have to say is not much, compared with the middle ages and antiquity, it is still better to remain in our sphere and to renounce all sorts of mystical theories which will not be visualized or experienced by anybody.[1]

I heard a man say in a regional conference some

[1] Peter Hammond, *Liturgy and Architecture* (London, 1960), p. 55.

months ago (jointly sponsored by the churches of Toronto, Canada, and the Department of Church Building and Architecture of the National Council of Churches) that

> The real ornament of the church is the action which takes place within it. If this action is missing, or not right, the church room will have no significant ornament.

Somewhere in the planning, the church and the architect must think about the relationship of the church building to the community. Exactly what this will be takes its direction from the things we have just been talking about. *Architecture can be defined as the fixing of relationships in space.* Professor J. A. Whyte, a theologian of the Church of Scotland, has this to say on this issue:

> . . . what are the relationships which the theologian is asking the architect to express in spatial terms. It is convenient to distinguish external and internal relationships.
>
> External relationships; i.e., the relationship of the building to its environment. In the case of the Church, this must rest upon the relation of the worshipping community to the community in which it is set.[2]

He cites two examples: One in which the church building sits four-square on its little hill in the midst of the town and seems both externally and internally to symbolize the whole community — i.e., the whole civil community gathered around word and sacrament, both matrix and offspring of the community! "And this was not simply ideal, it was reality. Here church and com-

[2] J. A. Whyte, The Theological Basis of Church Architecture (A paper prepared for the New Churches Research Group Conference at St. Andrew's, Scotland, April 6, 1961).

munity are one." [3] The second example is the manner in which we usually think of the great medieval cathedral, whose image, as Peter Hammond says, still haunts us. What relationship between Church and community did the medieval cathedral symbolize? Hammond quotes the answer of an American Roman Catholic bishop. "It typified wealth and power and esteem, if not downright human pride. It chose mass and bulk and height . . . the greater the mass and the more exalted the height, the more impressive the symbolism. . . . All this however, had very little relation to actual usefulness, for the cathedral quite obviously was not designed to house the family of God." [4]

This raises questions, Professor Whyte says, but states that he is interested in asking simply, "Ought the Church to dominate?" He quotes the Statement of the 1959 Ecumenical Conference on Architecture and the Church which says that the serving and not the dominating role of the Church should be kept in mind. This, he writes, would seem to be more Christian, and in terms of economics, a more attainable value, but it is clear that the two solutions of the external relationship is a live option in our modern secularized world. [5]

Reinhold's suggestion is relevant here. He asks:

> How much of a church's visible form should be dedicated to cosmic or religious symbolism and how much to its main purpose: the celebration of the liturgy — the particular liturgy of its age and its geographic location? [6]

The questions we have been quoting introduce a

[3] *Ibid.*

[4] Hammond, *op. cit.*, p. 165.

[5] Whyte, *op. cit.*

[6] H. A. Reinhold, "Liturgy and Church Architecture," *Jubilee* (Feb., 1962), p. 17.

matter of serious concern which it is essential in our planning to inspect from every angle.

> . . . what is the shape of the congregational life, and its relation to the community? Has the church to be the center of community life, or should it serve and leven the secular life of the community? Should it be gathering its members in the church buildings for their social life, or sending them out into secular organizations? Is the church to be apart from the community or a part of the community? . . . Two things may be said. First, the Church which is the Church of Jesus Christ, of Him who came not to be ministered unto but to minister, and to give His life a ransom for many, will express values that are at odds with many of the values round about it — in the new roadhouse, for instance. Secondly, this foreign-ness must not be understood as if it were an anachronism or a hangover from earlier and nicer days. It is tragic if the suspicion with which many people start (that the Church is simply an anachronistic survival providing a comforting escape for those who find the modern world too frightening or insecure) is confirmed by the kind of building we erect. The Church as a community, it seems to me, can only live in the time and in the culture in which it is set. We cannot reject modern culture, yearning for a golden age in the past; that is impossible, for whether we like it or not, we are modern men; and it is wrong, for our God is a living God, and not a dead God . . . not only the Lord of all that is good in our mastery of nature and of techniques, He is the judge of all our false standards and values.[7]

Professor Whyte believes that "it cannot be too strongly stressed that a modern church must be as much an example of modern architecture and belong to the

[7] Whyte, *op. cit.*

modern community as a modern shopping center. . . The building will be recognizable as a church when it successfully expresses what our idea of the Church is in its relationship to the modern world." [8]

In dealing with the internal relationships, Professor Whyte, of course, strikes another blow for the now familiar position that the worship of the community (the corporate worship of the people of God gathered about the word and the sacraments) must shape the spaces. This involves the freeing of the holy table from a remote area in a bicameral room to a location closer to the congregation gathered in a unicameral room. Every provision is to be made to encourage the participant relationship and discourage the spectator relationship. These are familiar matters now and I will not dwell on them. My point is that it is essential in good planning for the church room that all of these things be carefully thought about.

In leaving this area of our discussion, I cannot resist quoting our friend, Edward Sövik, architect of Northfield, Minnesota, who had a great thing to say in this connection at the 1960 Fall Retreat of the Department of Church Building and Architecture and the Church Architectural Guild of America:

> I think it is necessary also, to say something about the Christian ethic as it may be reflected in architecture.
>
> There is the temptation among people who become absorbed with the fascinating problems of systematic theology to forget temporarily that the greatest thing in the world is not faith or hope, but *love*. And among those of us who have inclinations to scoff at the pseudo-Gothic or pseudo-Colonial, it is

[8] *Ibid.*

easy to forget that these churches were also built out of love and that some of them actually have the qualities of architecture which are very kind to people, gentler and friendlier and more compassionate than many of the more honest and vigorous contemporary churches.

I do not mean to say that it is not possible to design a church that is kind and at the same time new and disciplined, and consistent with precepts of architectural integrity and dogmatic truth. Indeed, the devotion to truth is one aspect of love, and that love is not complete which evades discipline, or honesty, or truth, at *any* level.

But I do mean to say that whatever else our churches are, they ought also to be ministers of compassion and sympathy. They must not be proud, or detached or inhuman; they must not be monuments which impose themselves on people.

I come now to the end of my paper. You have been patient; I am thankful. Let me in closing attempt a summary of those things I spoke about which I believe the church building committee people must do in basic planning:

Building committees must know how to organize and how to manage the building program to the end that the building program will be resolved in the Lord's favor and the building will serve the church's task in the community. Building committees must evaluate the church's mission in terms of the activities that must be housed and their relation to each other and to the community and describe it all so precisely that the building will be exactly related to its Christian work and witness. They must know their theological position and the social context in which they plan to build. They must know above everything what their business is and how their role differs from that of the architect and of others who will play a part in the undertaking. They must know how to talk to architects and work with them and with artists, builders, craftsmen, engineers *and* the congregation.

There can be no evocative, instrumental, authentically communicative church building without a congregation that knows what it believes and knows what it wants to do about what it believes in today's world, and finds an architect who may not be the cheapest or the most expensive but who comprehends the true dimensions of the problem and can go as far with it as it is architecturally possible.